Playgrounds for Free

The Utilization of Used and Surplus Materials in Playground Construction

Paul Hogan

The MIT Press
Cambridge, Massachusetts, and London, England

Copyright © 1974 by
The Massachusetts Institute of Technology

This book was designed and produced by the MIT Press Media Department,
edited by Ed Agro and proofread by Mary Slocum,
typed in IBM Selectric Elite 72 by Mary Lou Supple,
printed and bound by Semline Inc.
in the United States of America

Library of Congress Cataloging in Publication Data

Hogan, Paul.
 Playgrounds for free.

 1. Playgrounds. 2. Playgrounds - Apparatus and equipment.
I. Title.
GV424.H63   790'.068   74-20514
ISBN 0-262-08078-8

For
Miss Betty
(Elizabeth Foster Stonorov)
Oskar Stonorov
and
Charles Lennox

3

How to Do It, How Not to Do It

MILTON J. SHAPP
GOVERNOR

July 1, 1974

For more than a dozen years, I have been associated with Paul
Hogan and his unique playground building techniques. In the early
sixties, he worked and built playgrounds in all sections of
Philadelphia. As the then President of Neighborhood Renewal Corps,
I relied on Paul to work with community groups to construct play-
grounds out of recycled materials.

We helped develop the Land Utilization Program of the City of
Philadelphia, which prompted the recycling of land for community
playgrounds. We learned much in those early days.

On becoming Governor in 1971, I asked Paul to renew his efforts
at building playgrounds. He has worked diligently with the
Pennsylvania Department of Community Affairs in promoting our concept of building playgrounds with people rather than for people.

We found from experience that when people in a neighborhood
are themselves involved in the planning process, the playground
is more readily accepted and becomes an integral part of the community. Many times playgrounds are built and not fully used, just
because the community was not involved in the planning stage.
When it becomes part of the planning process in the neighborhood,
it becomes part of the community life.

More than 125 playgrounds have been built in all parts of the
Commonwealth under Paul's "Playgrounds for Free" program.

I recommend this book heartily and hope that the program can
be spread nationwide. Paul has already lectured or built playgrounds in Connecticut, Wisconsin, Kansas, Tennessee and Alabama.
I am proud to have had a part in initiating this worthwhile community effort.

MILTON J. SHAPP
Governor

Introduction: What This Book Is About

The following pages are taken up, for the most part, by photographs of playground equipment being crawled over, sat upon, swung from, and otherwise used by children. This equipment, as can be seen, is constructed from the material castoffs of our society - old cable reels; superannuated telephone poles; bins and boxes; tires and tubes resurrected by the breath of fresh air without and within. In Parts 1 and 2 I show how to obtain such materials and how to build playgrounds out of them. I show how specific items may be constructed, and indicated the sorts of help one will need - and where to get it - in assembling and placing the larger constructions.

But there is a larger purpose to these demonstrations, which I hope the reader will perceive; this is to encourage individuals to expand their own inventiveness, both material and social. I feel that I have only scratched the surface of that vast and growing pile of industrial "junk" that can be used with profit in playgrounds; I am sure that there are many more ways than I have given here for people to take a hand in the construction and maintenance of their neighborhood playgrounds, and more stratagems whereby to encourage the officials of towns, public utilities, and industries to lend machine- and man-power to such projects. This book can only serve to point out resources and spur people on to go after them!

So a sharp eye will discover the raw materials, and a sharp wit will discover how to pull people together to convert those materials into a playground. But the building of a playground is only half the story, and the easier half at that. More difficult to accomplish is the nurturing of the playground - nurturing that must, in fact, be provided for as one of the very first things, even before the playground is actually completed. With such nurturing, the playground becomes an important, productive part of the community, and one that endures a span of time that is appropriate to its circumstances. I address this problem of nurture in Part 3. I recount, not only my past successes, but also my failures. The failures of various projects of the Neighborhood Renewal Corps taught me the great lesson: that the true social utility of a project is embedded in the degree of participation felt by the members of the community for whom the project is intended, and that success is directly related to the responsibility exercised by (sometimes, wrested by!) those beneficiaries. For a playground to succeed, its ultimate users must be its builders. This does not mean only that the adults of a community must build and be responsible for that community's playground; it also means that the children must be involved.

I used to think that I wanted to built playgrounds _for_ people; then I thought that I would build _with_ people; but now I see that by far the best - though most difficult - way is to encourage people to build _for themselves_.

In Part 3 I illustrate successful people-oriented playgrounds, as well as unsuccessful maintenance-oriented ones, that I have found on my travels. Many sorts of playgrounds are described in this book: from parking lots given over to the people after hours, through affairs built by those few city governments that, marvelous to relate, seem to perceive the active, necessary part children have in the life of the community; from experiments of community-minded individuals and groups who have taken matters into their own hands in those towns whose public servants seem to have no idea of the potential of the people, through the exciting concept of the adventure playground.

Any of these - and endless variations upon them - are available to citizens
willing to get their hands dirty, and who allow their children to get dirty
too, in the playground-building process.

The epitome of the theory of playgrounds is the idea of the adventure playground.
I devote relatively little space to this idea only because it has been covered
so well by Lady Allen and Arvid Bengtsson. Sad to say, America is years
behind England and other parts of the world in the playground movement. But
it should be clear to readers and viewers of this book that a playground for
free can be an adventure playground as well. The critical element, as
always, is the presence of adults who can draw the most out of their
"charges"; who, while taking care for the safety and capabilities of
children, can dare to let the children take charge of their own environment.

So, finally, this book is a description of some of the stepping-stones I've
trod on the way to those ultimate playgrounds built and rebuilt numberless
times by children.

1

Materials

Cable Reels

Chrissy Sanders inspecting hundreds of cable reels abandoned in a Philadelphia storage yard. Ten years ago I asked the owner of the yard to give us a few of the reels for playgrounds. He asked $75.00 each, so we got ours elsewhere for free. Now the owner's reels are rotten and rat-infested; and he must pay to have them hauled to the dump. How many cable reels are languishing in your city?

Next to tires, cable reels are the most
versatile and easy to obtain playground
building materials. They can be used to roll
heavy utility poles over long distances.
In our own tree house a small one serves as
the pulley for the elevator. Several recreation
departments use them for physical training
and balance development. If you put a steel
plate on top and hang a large reel on a
4-foot pole, you have an instant merry-go-
round.

During a demonstration of Playgrounds for
Free in the main square of Wilkes-Barre,
the local utility brought in an 8-foot
diameter cable reel. Within twenty-five
minutes, we had made it into a two-story
playhouse. The core had a thick wooden
spreader. With a chain saw, I cut doors and
windows in the reel. A swarm of kids
painted the house in just minutes with paint
donated by Sherwin Williams.

The main thing is to get the reels together.
The ideas will come thick and fast if you
have a brainstorming session. Perhaps
a local contest could be organized to design
new uses for cable reels. If you come up
with any good ones, let me know about it.

This bus stop shelter in Oil City, Pa., was built by Charles Welms, a retired
oil company employee. Waiting for the bus are Scott Carter, Johnny Riley, and
Duane Carter. Notice the window for bad weather look-out. It helps to bolt such
constructions down; otherwise they might roll away on Halloween.

Short stubs of utility poles keep this cable reel car from moving around at night. Constructions as heavy as this should not be designed to be pushed around unless there is adequate adult supervision.

This hot rod was built near Pittsfield, Ma., from cable reel ends, brass bedposts, and other parts picked up at the local junkyard.

Evangelina Garza spins Rachel Martinez on a merry-go-round made from a surplus cable reel end in the Guadalupe section of Phoenix, Az. The playground was designed and put together by architecture students of Arizona State University in cooperation with the children and adult residents of Guadalupe.

The Parks and Recreation Department of Greensboro, N.C., uses discarded cable reels in its physical fitness program. By riding the reels, the children develop coordination while having lots of fun. The children painted the reels shown here.

One of the vest pocket parks in Philadelphia used cable reels cut in half for part of a junior obstacle course.

VISTA volunteers from the Architect's Workshop in Pittsburgh built this cable reel assembly for the 1972 Three Rivers Arts Festival in downtown Pittsburgh. The children jumped off the reels onto a pile of foam rubber.

On my way to the Playgrounds for Free program, I spotted a big plank in the middle of the highway. I stopped and threw it onto my truck. On the capitol lawn I made a wagon, using some plastic pipe for axles, tiny cable wheels, and the plank for the body.

This tropical traffic policeman's stand was built by Gordon MacKenzie for the "Greening of Ruppert" adventure playground in New York City. Two sizes of reels were used and pipe welding was necessary for the braces.

8

The Canadian log roller was made from two cable reels with slats to form a log. With a steel-pipe axle, it ran so fast that no one could stay on board for more than three seconds.

To my knowledge, this was the first merry-go-round built from a cable reel. It was put together in Melon Park, Philadelphia, in the early sixties. Now there are ones like it all over Pennsylvania.

Plans for a cable reel merry-go-round. The size of the reel to be used depends upon the size of the children that the merry-go-round is installed for.

MERRY-GO-ROUND

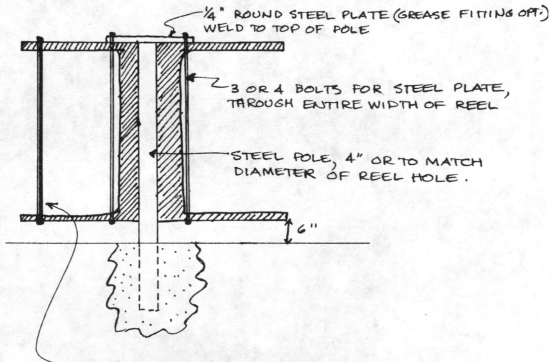

¼" ROUND STEEL PLATE (GREASE FITTING OPT.) WELD TO TOP OF POLE

3 OR 4 BOLTS FOR STEEL PLATE, THROUGH ENTIRE WIDTH OF REEL

STEEL POLE, 4" OR TO MATCH DIAMETER OF REEL HOLE.

6"

4-6 GRASPING POLES FOR THE CHILDREN MAY BE BOLTED 6-8" FROM EDGE OF REEL, AROUND ENTIRE CIRCUMFERENCE

Plans for the cable reel seesaw. I've made some seesaws by taking a slat out of the core of the reel and moving three or four slats so that I have two narrow slots. By inserting the board and bolting down, you have a very neat-looking seesaw.

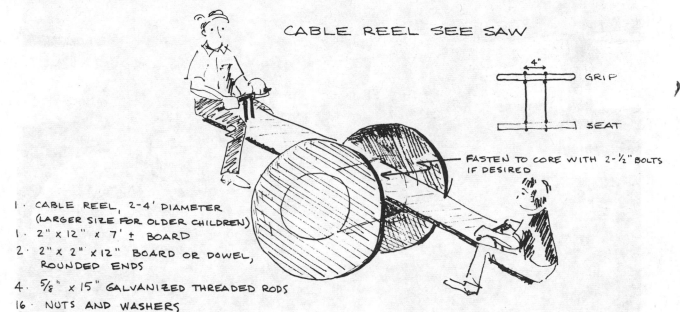

CABLE REEL SEE SAW

GRIP

SEAT

FASTEN TO CORE WITH 2-½" BOLTS
IF DESIRED

1 · CABLE REEL, 2-4' DIAMETER
    (LARGER SIZE FOR OLDER CHILDREN)
1 · 2" x 12" x 7' ± BOARD
2 · 2" x 2" x 12" BOARD OR DOWEL,
    ROUNDED ENDS
4 · ⅝" x 15" GALVANIZED THREADED RODS
16 · NUTS AND WASHERS

The children of Casey Park, the Wilkes-Barre flood disaster trailer site, called this assembly "Mushroom City." The park was built by VISTA volunteers, working with the author and the Pennsylvania Department of Community Affairs. The ladder is made from several pallets bolted together. In fact, all the materials were bolted for stability and hence safety. The Park was bulldozed to make a baseball field in 1973.

SPOOL TOWER

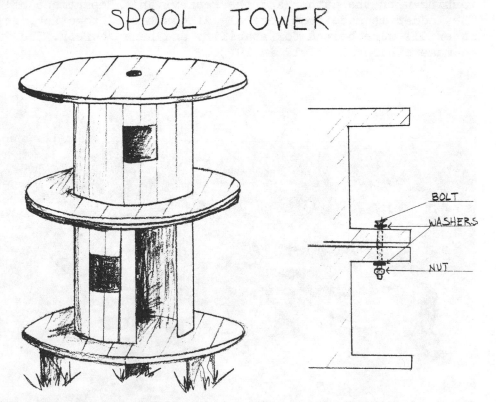

BOLT

WASHERS

NUT

Playground at the Steelton, Pa., flood disaster trailer park. VISTA volunteers and the children of the park assembled this playground in less than two hours.

Plans for the cable reel tower. Such constructions last a few years longer if you get them off the ground, as shown.

CABLE REEL CASTLE

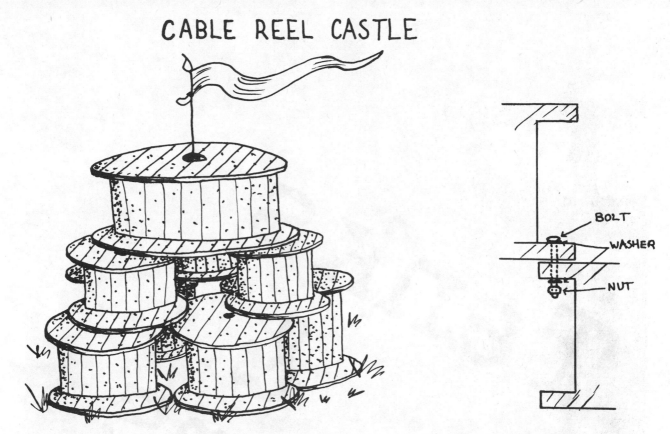

The plans for a cable reel castle are pretty much the same as for the tower, except that any and all sizes of reels can be used. Just make sure they are all bolted together. If there is a space between some reels, fill it with 2 x 4's or other appropriate shims.

"Dracula's Castle" was built in Casey Park. Granger Brown, VISTA volunteer from Tennessee, working with the Department of Community Affairs, built this playspace with the help of "Granger's Rangers" - other VISTA volunteers and the children of Casey.

Tanks & Drums

If there's a friendly welder in you neighborhood, he can create a very nice lightweight tunnel-slide out of several oil drums welded end to end. Make sure he smooths down the sharp edges.

Who can possibly think of all the uses
tanks and drums can be put to?
You can make bucking broncos, dugout shelters
for baseball teams, huge rolling swings,
tunnels, space heaters and water heaters,
fireplaces, floats for rafts, and a thousand
other things both useful and playful.

A 250-gallon oil tank makes a very good boiler for the engine of this old
train in the Carolina trailer park in Wilkes-Barre. See pages 160, 161 for
more about this Carolina Choo Choo.

Tanks are a drug on the market. How often have you seen piles of them scattered throughout the city? Every empty lot has its share and no one puts them to use. Well, almost no one. I have photos of how they are used in different parts of the world and drawings of how they can be recycled for a second life. They are easy to get for the hauling, especially if they have pinhole leaks in them. It's easy to either weld such holes shut or insert self-tapping screws, which cost five cents each.

This oil tank dugout was inspired by an ad I saw in the papers about how to recycle oil tanks, now that natural gas is available. You could probably talk your local oil distributer into cutting up a few and donating them to your cause. They don't do him any good if they have small leaks, and he can write the donation off the charity. Cut the tanks with a torch or a steel-cutting blade on an electric circular saw. Make sure to file down the rough edges or bend them over. And drill a few drain holes in the bottom or you'll have an unwanted swimming pool in your shelter.

OIL TANK DUGOUT

I'd like to see an outdoor music playground.
Various sized drums could be sunk into the
ground. Each drum could be tuned to a certain
pitch, either by the depth, the size, or the
fullness. Then anyone could come along and
bang away and soon children would bang away
in rhythm.

This bucking bronco, made from a 55-gallon oil drum suspended from four
surplus utility poles, is in almost constant use at the Rawhide camp/home
for disadvantaged boys in New London, Wi. Chains anchor it to the ground so
that it won't buck too much when the motive power (supplied by the boy on
the right) is applied. By working the tug-line, the boy can tilt the bronc or
make it go forward or backward, up or down; and it can even be made to roll.

Rudolph Ilich plays on a "watchamacalit" made of old tires, an oil drum,
cables, and steel piping. The sort-of-bronco is in a people's park in Chicago.
A lot was cleaned and the park built by the Young Lords and the Concerned
Puerto Rican Youth Organization.

I'd build a super guitar using old piano wires
and a steel drum base. I'd also include wind
instruments. The wind organ could be made
of large pipes and drums, and the wind could
come from a huge fan cranked by one or two
children. The kids themselves could act
as stops to the organ pipes.

Can you imagine the beautiful noise and rhythm
from such an outdoor band which could
withstand the elements and vandals and
produce beautiful music?

Horses in a playground in Luanda, Angola, made from old oil drums and steel
pipe legs. Note the welding, as well as woodwork, required for such a project.
Just outside of Johnstown, Pa., I saw this young lady waiting for the school
bus. Her father made the shelter from an old 500-gallon fuel oil tank.

Concrete

pipe

A row of new sewer pipes awaiting installation provides a temporary play site.

Concrete pipe manufacturers have mountains of
cracked, chipped, or less than perfect pipe
which cannot be sold, but which is still
serviceable for use in playgrounds.
Playgrounds and recreational facilities all
over the world, in poor communities as well
as in wealthy ones, are constantly looking
for these pipes for their play areas. It is
too difficult in most cases to get city hall
to purchase them and playground organizers
can't see how to get them any other way.

A chipped oval concrete pipe provides a retreat for Richard Abraham, Kim Eadie,
and Steve Ardes at the Charlestown Playhouse. You won't find adults bothering
the kids in this sort of hideaway.

Meanwhile, army and navy yards and local
and state government maintenance depots are
clogged with cranes, tractors and flatbed
trailers, bulldozers, and all sorts of other
material-handling equipment which in most
cases is used just a few days a month.

Why can't the army or city hall release a low-bed rig with a driver for one day a month to go to the pipe manufacturer, who in turn will gladly load it up with huge pipes for free delivery to nonprofit recreational facilities? The pipe manufacturer's prayers will be answered as his useless surplus is hauled away free to where it can help people and yet not cut into his market. Neighborhood groups who work together to build a playground will welcome the pipe with open arms.

This cliff-dwellers' unit was designed by Professor Peter Spooner of the Architecture Faculty, University of New South Wales, Australia. The pre-fab sewer junction boxes were assembled by the Brisbane Public Works Department.

This pipe situation can be extended to almost any sort of building material imaginable. The excess concrete resulting from safety-factor over-orders on big jobs is just dumped in a huge pile at the ready-mix plant. The contractor, if shown the tax advantages of donating this surplus, should be glad to donate it to the communities' benefit.

This playground in Takahama, on the Noto Peninsula of Japan, uses concrete pipe and boxes for a train. Cutting the pipe with a concrete-cutting blade on an electric saw, to provide windows, requires lots of elbow grease and patching cement.

Further up the Noto Peninsula, in Wajima, this little play area was constructed by bulldozing a pile of rubble over some concrete pipes and adding a few half-buried tires. Flat rocks laid on the hillside prevent erosion.

The same goes for surplus fire engines, ropes, ladders, and almost anything else put together by man. If you can prove that it is profitable for him to donate cast-off materials, you'll make an environmentalist out of the most hard-hearted businessman.

Note:

When designing play equipment made of concrete pipe, do not give into the temptation to make use of the rollability of the pipe. Concrete is heavy! That's one reason why, when securely anchored, it is a safe material for playground use. But, by the same token, <u>unanchored</u> or free-rolling pipe is most dangerous, and should not be part of your playground.

The Department of Amenities of Salisbury, Rhodesia, constructed what must be the largest snake in all of Africa.

A critical eye for safety should be cast on your other designs using heavy timbers, old autos, etc. If there is a person in your neighborhood with competence in this area, try to convince him or her to act as the "safety person" of your group. And look to see that poles, pipes, and other heavy items cannot be pushed over or rolled about. Get the utility or industrial workers who are helping you to think of this problem while they work, and to dig deep!

Concrete pipes aren't just for carrying gunk or to crawl through. The North Meadows Apartment Residents Recreation Committee in Milwaukee, Wi., sponsored a "paint the pipe" contest. Contestants Claudia Weaver, Scott Luebke, Claudia's sister Lora, and Luke Belsito are shown admiring their handiwork. This is a positive expression of graffiti.

The designer of this school playground in Denmark must have had a great load of free concrete pipes and forms, but used them imaginatively in building see-through, climb-over, walk-on-top-of walls. Concrete test cores and interlocking concrete blocks hold back sand, and other concrete cylinders and slabs make a nice sitting area near the classrooms.

The deaf children of the Listening Eyes School in Columbus, Ga., use large concrete pipes for their classrooms while they listen to their teachers through special radios and earphones. The special education school uses all sorts of cast-off materials in its playground - from tires to climbers made from old utility poles (see page 241).

Utility poles

At the University School in Milwaukee, a pupil carefully picks his way along a stump clump. There are few things simpler or cheaper than logs from a dead tree stuck into the ground, though digging the holes requires lots of effort.

An alpine walk is easily built by spacing the poles apart and at different angles. You should plant them one foot deep for every two feet out of the ground.

Youths from Project Interchange, the Seattle Schools' alternative program, sit victoriously atop their climber. The assembly had been torn down by a rival gang a week before. The builders went back, dug deeper, added a dozen more poles, and did the job super right. When they saw the apparatus rebuilt with double the strength, the other kids turned their anger to respect and cooperation.

Utility poles are probably the most common
and useful of all cast-off building materials.
Everywhere there is electricity there are
utility poles. Even after the utilities use
the poles for thirty or forty years, there
are still scores of years left in them. Up
until recently, if the cause was worthy, most
utility companies were more than glad to not
only donate the poles, but deliver them,
dig the holes with their auger machines, and
set them as well!

Inflation and a growing wood shortage - new
poles, that cost the utilities $20 each in
1973, now cost $90 and have to be imported
from Finland - are leading to a scarcity of
used poles. But these are still around; be
persistent, and you will find them.

Some utility companies have their own sawmills,
where they cut up the poles for blocking and
pallets. The sawmill rejects make fine fencing.
Philadelphia Electric Company has been most
generous in many of my projects. They have
helped with swing assemblies, bridges, sand

boxes, and all sorts of projects. The
contributions of Philadelphia Electric are
scattered throughout this book.

The uses for old poles in playgrounds are
endless. You can make swings, dividers,
animals, rollers, bridges, tripods, and just
about anything else you can imagine. Just get
a few poles, and ideas will pop into your
head faster than you can cut the poles up to
make playground equipment.

CLIMBING PYRAMID

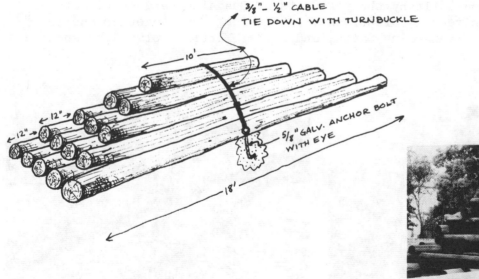

This drawing of a utility climbing pyramid is after a design by the Oregon
State Highway Commission. Just make sure the poles are well anchored so they
don't roll over on children while they are scaling the pyramid.

Professor Peter Spooner of the Faculty of Architecture of the University of
New South Wales, Australia, designed this climbing maze of poles for the
Randwick Municipal Council. Council workmen made sure that the construction
wouldn't shift by driving long spikes into the poles.

LOG FORT

9' SQUARE MINIMUM
8' POSTS OR RAILROAD TIES, 12" DIAM. MINIMUM
SINK POSTS 2'6"
HORIZONTAL LOGS 10"-12" DIAM., VARYING LENGTHS

SHORTER POSTS OF VARYING HEIGHTS MAY BE
SUNK BOTH INSIDE AND OUTSIDE FOR CLIMBING.

This is a redrawn version of a log fort by W. A. Mikulsky of Canada. Be sure the top rails are well anchored.

In Brisbane there is a novel truss bridge in Peter Spooner's playground. Note the use of utility poles, cross arms, and long timbers for the deck.

This is part of the Guadalupe Community Recreation area in Phoenix, Az. The park was designed and built by the residents of Guadalupe and architecture students from the University of Arizona. On the long "get together and love" pole Terry Martinez, Evangeline Garza, and Rachel Martinez play a balance game.

CABLE WALK

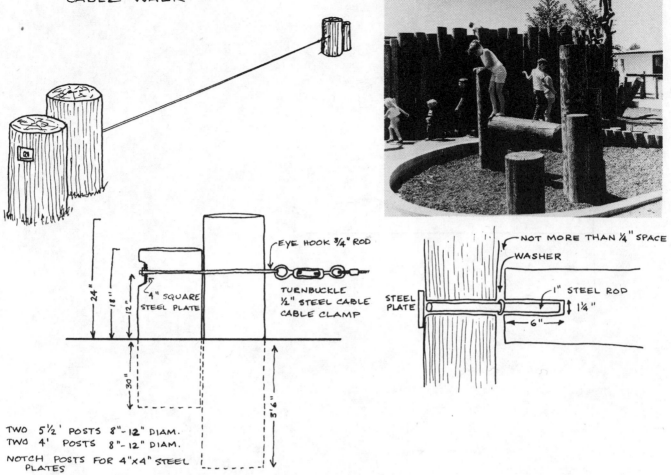

EYE HOOK ¾" ROD

TURNBUCKLE
½" STEEL CABLE
CABLE CLAMP

4" SQUARE
STEEL PLATE

24"
18"
12"

30"

3'6"

TWO 5½' POSTS 8"-12" DIAM.
TWO 4' POSTS 8"-12" DIAM.
NOTCH POSTS FOR 4"x4" STEEL PLATES

NOT MORE THAN ¼" SPACE
WASHER
1" STEEL ROD
1¼"
6"
STEEL PLATE

This is a good design for a tightrope or cable walk. This device gives children a good opportunity to develop their balance skills safely. It's very important to set the cable alongside a hedge, wall, or fence; otherwise, some one may run into it and trip. A heavy-duty turnbuckle is necessary to maintain the proper tension.

This roller poller was designed by Theodore Osmundson, past president of the American Society of Landscape Architects, for the John F. Baldwin Park in Concord, Ca. It looks quite simple, but the roller pole must be very straight and true; otherwise, an erratic roll is the result. You could add pipe sleeves to the 1" steel rod to provide a faster ride.

The tether ball assembly can be easily made from an eight-foot piece of utility pole. Be sure it is anchored at least three feet in the ground.

TETHER BALL

1- 8' POLE
LAG SCREW EYE BOLT
ROPE
TETHER BALL

BALANCING BEAMS

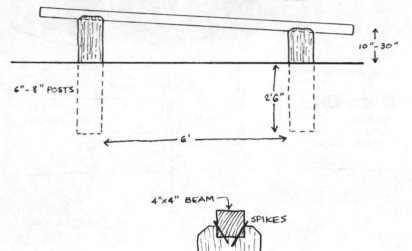

4"x4" BEAM
10 FEET LONG

10"-30"

6"-8" POSTS

2'6"

6'

4"x4" BEAM

SPIKES

Many parents and teachers want balance beams of this sort to help develop the motor skills of their children. I built one such device with mostly left turns because the children seemed to be less agile in making this maneuver.

A variation of the balance beam, the pole mountain was encountered at a small school on the Noto Peninsula on Honshu, Japan. I have used these in many combinations in the playgrounds of Pennsylvania.

POLE MOUNTAIN

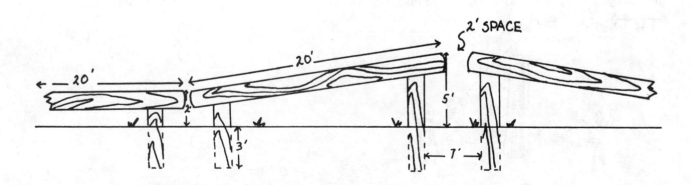

2' SPACE

20'

20'

5'

3'

7'

UTILITY POLE BENCH/WALK/DIVIDER

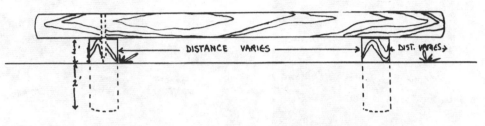

½" I.D. (¾" O.D.) PIPE CONNECTOR

SAW FLAT PART FROM HORIZONTAL
POLE TO FIT ON TOP

SECTION OF POST

DISTANCE VARIES — DIST. VARIES

This utility pole bench/walk/divider is just that. The elevation determines its use. It can be a soft bench, a place for children to balance-walk, or a divider to keep cars where they belong. You notch either the top pole or the post. A section of water pipe does a good job of holding the poles together.

CANTILEVER TIRE SWING

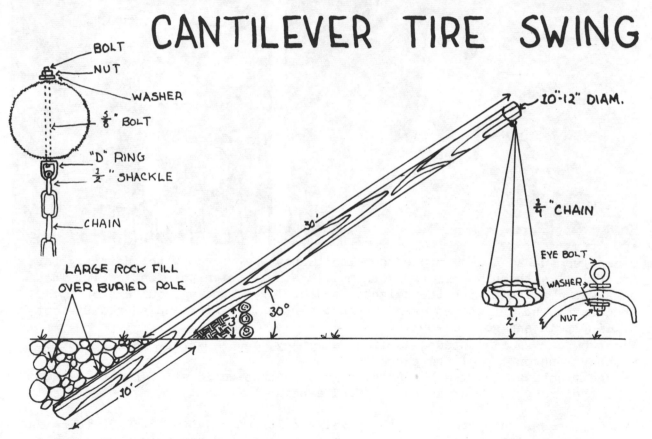

BOLT
NUT
WASHER
⅝" BOLT
"D" RING
½" SHACKLE
CHAIN

LARGE ROCK FILL
OVER BURIED POLE

30'
30°
10'

10"-12" DIAM.

¾" CHAIN

EYE BOLT
WASHER
2'
NUT

This cantilever tire swing is after a design by John Cook, a landscape architect in Rockford, Il. Playground Clearing House, Inc. has made dozens around the state of Pennsylvania, and these swings are far superior to conventional ones. A child is soon bored by swinging alone in a private swing seat and there is always a minor crisis when others want their turn. With a horizontal tire swing four or five children can all ride at once. These swings go forward and backward and sideways, and spin around on the swivel.

Once a woman had a dead maple she didn't know what to do with. Her neighbor, an artist, with only a little work made a simple totem pole out of it. This pole was a big hit with the neighborhood children, and was quite enough for the woman. The artist, however, was not content. So he found an old 25-foot-long utility pole and got to work.

First he carved his totems - a lion, a monkey, and a parrot. Then he put a weather vane on top of the parrot's head.

The next job was to find a special base coat that would allow him to paint over the creosote. Then he had to find a paint that would go over the base coat.

Finally he was ready to raise the pole. A contractor wanted $150.00 to raise it, so the artist called up ten of his neighbors, and together they did the job themselves.

As can be seen from the small construction, it's not necessary to carve deeply in order to have an attractive totem pole. Still, the most important element in a totem-pole project is an adult who can teach the children the patient and safe use of tools and paint.

um Budapester Platz (Budapest Plaza Children's Play
ourg, Germany, went all out in building a beautiful pole
he sand levels between each tier of poles provide unlimited
ity and are soft enough for jumping.

The Honolulu Park Department prevailed on the local utility company to
transfer some of their "trees" to one of their parks. This sort of realistic
apparatus can help form a child's conception of what those men are doing at
the top of high poles. It is much better than a plastic- or steel-pipe
simulated climber.

DINOSAUR TAIL SAND BOX

EXPOSE POLES 1' TO 4'
GRADUALLY ~ KEEPING 2'
UNDERGROUND

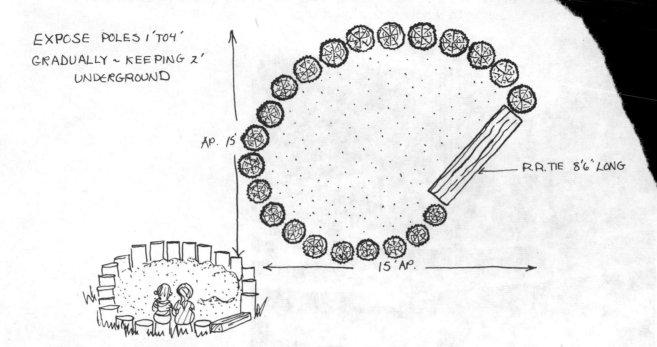

AP. 15'

R.R. TIE 8'6" LONG

15' AP.

SAND BOX

STEEL STRAP

3 · 20' POLES
3 · 4' PERFORATED STEEL STRAPS $\frac{3}{16}$" x $1\frac{1}{2}$"
    (NAILED TO POLES AT CORNERS)

Jane Mitchie designed this dinosaur tail sand box for the Central Elementary
School in Haddonfield, New Jersey. The best way to build one is to plant the
poles all at once. Then cut each pole with a chain saw, a few inches higher
than the previous one. A railroad tie between the ends keeps in the sand and
provides a nice seat for the children. Each child is given the freedom to
climb as high as he or she dares. The children jump into the sand at
ever-increasing heights, and thus develop their own perception of danger and
explore their right to risk.

A sandbox can be made from old poles. Perforated steel strapping and
forty-penny nails will hold the poles together, and they need no anchoring.
They won't go anywhere.

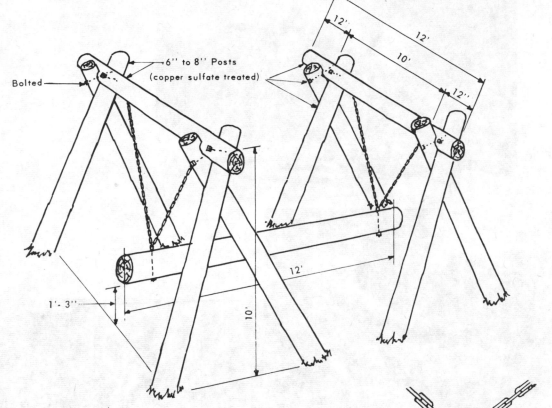

6" to 8" Posts
(copper sulfate treated)

Bolted

12'

12'

10'

12'

12'

1'- 3"

10'

Note—

1. Use natural stain for logs.

2. Fasten two chains to supporting log and attach to
eyebolt on swing log.

3. Notch logs where necessary and bolt together.

4. Treat poles below ground and sink 2 1/2 feet.

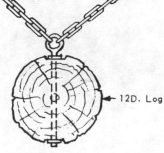

12D. Log

CROSS SECTION

THROUGH SWING LOG

Canada contributed a heavy duty ten-kid swing made with utility poles.

The students of Brian Woods, Assistant Professor of Architecture at the University of Manitoba, designed and built this cargo net climber several years ago and he reports that it is still as good as new. Note its similarity to the log swing. The use of heavy, spaced logs on the ground here eliminates the need for excavation work. Also note the recesses for the bolts, an important safety feature. The recesses were cut with a chain saw.

Utility poles bolted at odd angles provide a sturdy and beautiful play assembly. The heavy ship hawser and the pipe add to the follow-the-leader potential of the construction.

The Philadelphia Recreation Department built this pole complex with a lot of cargo nets and ropes to make the spider web climber. I have found it very difficult to get such nets, perhaps because skids and pallets are now used rather than nets.

UTILITY POLE BENCH/WALK/DIVIDER

½" I.D. (⅞" O.D.) PIPE CONNECTOR

SAW FLAT PART FROM HORIZONTAL
POLE TO FIT ON TOP

SECTION OF POST

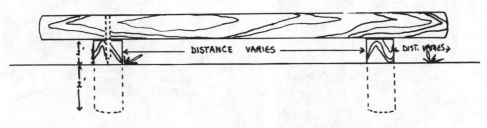

DISTANCE VARIES

DIST. VARIES

This utility pole bench/walk/divider is just that. The elevation determines
its use. It can be a soft bench, a place for children to balance-walk, or a
divider to keep cars where they belong. You notch either the top pole or the
post. A section of water pipe does a good job of holding the poles together.

CANTILEVER TIRE SWING

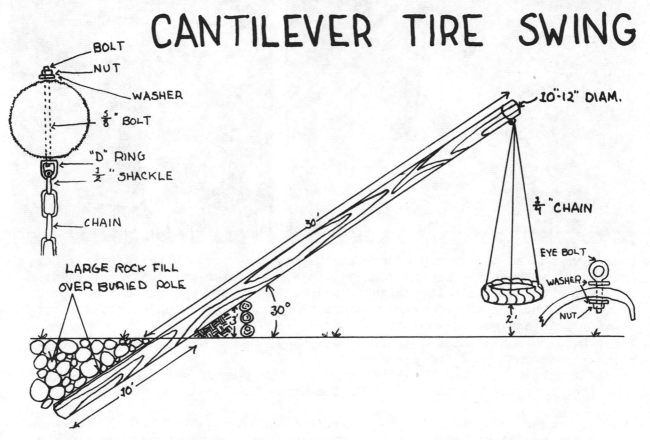

BOLT
NUT
WASHER
⅝" BOLT
"D" RING
½" SHACKLE
CHAIN

LARGE ROCK FILL
OVER BURIED POLE

30'

30°

10'

10"-12" DIAM.

¾" CHAIN

EYE BOLT
WASHER
NUT

2'

This cantilever tire swing is after a design by John Cook, a landscape
architect in Rockford, Il. Playground Clearing House, Inc. has made dozens
around the state of Pennsylvania, and these swings are far superior to
conventional ones. A child is soon bored by swinging alone in a private swing
seat and there is always a minor crisis when others want their turn. With a
horizontal tire swing four or five children can all ride at once. These swings
go forward and backward and sideways, and spin around on the swivel.

Once a woman had a dead maple she didn't know what to do with. Her neighbor, an artist, with only a little work made a simple totem pole out of it. This pole was a big hit with the neighborhood children, and was quite enough for the woman. The artist, however, was not content. So he found an old 25-foot-long utility pole and got to work.

First he carved his totems - a lion, a monkey, and a parrot. Then he put a weather vane on top of the parrot's head.

The next job was to find a special base coat that would allow him to paint over the creosote. Then he had to find a paint that would go over the base coat.

Finally he was ready to raise the pole. A contractor wanted $150.00 to raise it, so the artist called up ten of his neighbors, and together they did the job themselves.

As can be seen from the small construction, it's not necessary to carve deeply in order to have an attractive totem pole. Still, the most important element in a totem-pole project is an adult who can teach the children the patient and safe use of tools and paint.

The Kinderspielzentrum Budapester Platz (Budapest Plaza Children's Play Center) in Nuremburg, Germany, went all out in building a beautiful pole playground. The sand levels between each tier of poles provide unlimited play activity and are soft enough for jumping.

The Honolulu Park Department prevailed on the local utility company to transfer some of their "trees" to one of their parks. This sort of realistic apparatus can help form a child's conception of what those men are doing at the top of high poles. It is much better than a plastic- or steel-pipe simulated climber.

DINOSAUR TAIL SAND BOX

EXPOSE POLES 1' TO 4'
GRADUALLY ~ KEEPING 2'
        UNDERGROUND

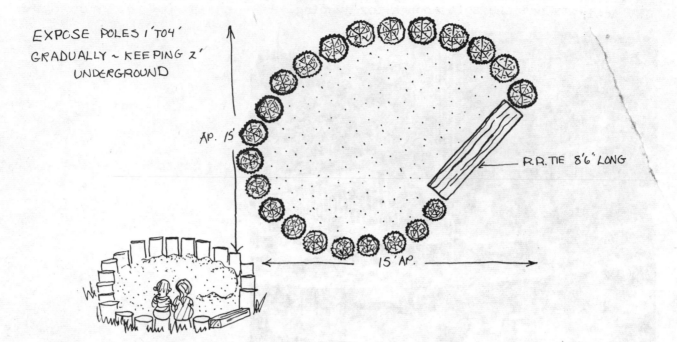

AP. 15'

R.R. TIE 8'6" LONG

15' AP.

SAND BOX

STEEL STRAP

3 · 20' POLES
3 · 4' PERFORATED STEEL STRAPS 3/16" x 1½"
        (NAILED TO POLES AT CORNERS)

Jane Mitchie designed this dinosaur tail sand box for the Central Elementary
School in Haddonfield, New Jersey. The best way to build one is to plant the
poles all at once. Then cut each pole with a chain saw, a few inches higher
than the previous one. A railroad tie between the ends keeps in the sand and
provides a nice seat for the children. Each child is given the freedom to
climb as high as he or she dares. The children jump into the sand at
ever-increasing heights, and thus develop their own perception of danger and
explore their right to risk.

A sandbox can be made from old poles. Perforated steel strapping and
forty-penny nails will hold the poles together, and they need no anchoring.
They won't go anywhere.

This revolving bronco seesaw was far and away the most popular piece of play equipment in Melon Park in Philadelphia. It was designed and built by a Venezuelan art student more than a dozen years ago. Of all the equipment made by him and his fellow students at the Philadelphia College or Art, this was the only one that held up. The Friends' Neighborhood Guild, the sponsors of the playground, made me take it away after a few weeks with the refrain, "The insurance company won't approve." It was the only thing that held the attention of the fifteen and sixteen year olds and I was as sad as they were when I had to remove it. From then on it was all downhill, and the playground practically self-destructed for lack of involvement and leadership. The children were soon back at their previous play of hopping on the rears of trolleys and trucks and jumping from rooftop to rooftop thirty feet in the air. Rather than throw the seesaw away, I brought it home and hundreds of kids have played on it these past twelve years. No one has ever been hurt. When the authorities tell you something can't be done because of "insurance," don't believe them. Most schools, cities, and organizations have blanket coverage and anything reasonable can be insured within the big policy. Call the insurance company yourself if you have any questions. Show them your ideas. Form a committee. Do it!

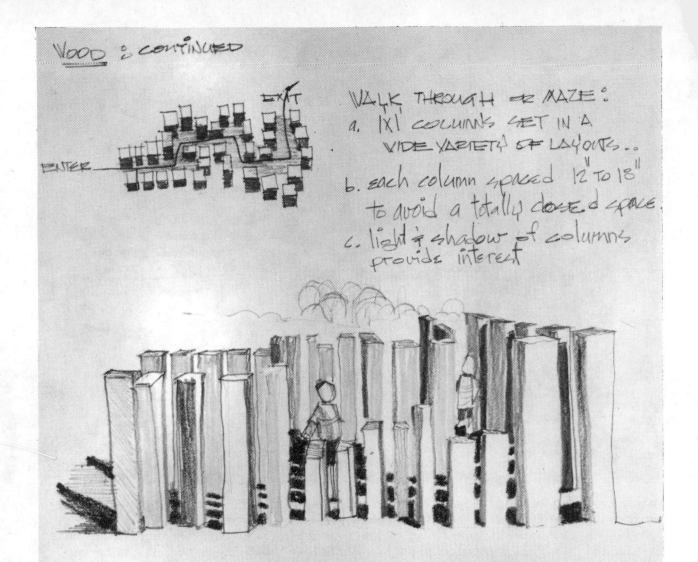

EXIT

ENTER

WALK THROUGH a MAZE:
a. 1X1 COLUMNS SET IN A
   WIDE VARIETY OF LAYOUTS..
b. each column spaced 12" to 18"
   to avoid a totally closed space.
c. light & shadow of columns
   provide interest

THE SKETCHES SHOWN ARE A PORTION
OF PLAYGROUND STUDIES BEING CARRIED ON
BY THE PLANNING DEPARTMENT OF THE
CORPUS CHRISTI, PARK & REC DEPARTMENT.

THESE FACILITIES HAVE NOT BEEN CONSTRUCTED
AS OF THIS WRITING...... PLANS ARE BEING
PREPARED TO BUILD WORKING UNITS IN THE
FUTURE.

M. DUDLEY
PARK PLANNER 5-28-70   4/4

These drawings by M. Dudley of Corpus Christi, Tx., illustrate ideas for
pole mazes. Railroad ties on end would provide a good maze for smaller
children. Also note that such a maze can be combined with a totem pole
forest.

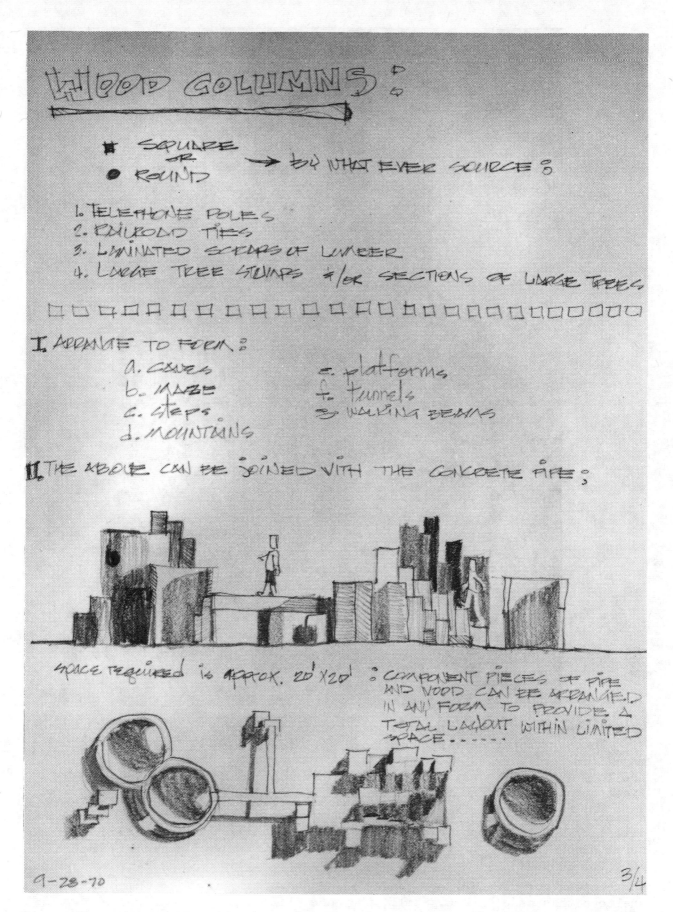

WOOD COLUMNS:

■ SQUARE
or
● ROUND → BY WHAT EVER SOURCE:

1. TELEPHONE POLES
2. RAILROAD TIES
3. LAMINATED SCRAPS OF LUMBER
4. LARGE TREE STUMPS #/or SECTIONS OF LARGE TREES

I ARRANGE TO FORM:
    a. caves
    b. MAZE
    c. steps.
    d. MOUNTAINS

    e. platforms
    f. tunnels
    g. WALKING BEAMS

II THE ABOVE CAN BE JOINED WITH THE CONCRETE PIPE:

SPACE REQUIRED is APPROX. 20'X20' : COMPONENT PIECES OF PIPE AND WOOD CAN BE ARRANGED IN ANY FORM TO PROVIDE A TOTAL LAYOUT WITHIN LIMITED SPACE......

9-28-70

3/4

Yet another M. Dudley sketch, here showing the combination of a pole maze and other shapes.

What do foresters do during those long winter months? Men of the Grand Rapids, Mi., Forestry Department put their skills to use in building play equipment made from dead oaks and maples. The logs run from two to six feet long. Note the long drill bit. Only the rough edges are taken off the constructions. Final smoothing is done free of charge by the youngsters playing on them.

A simple log ladder can be built with four base poles four or five inches in diameter. The rungs can be two inches thick. Just bolt them securely being sure to countersink the bolts. Don't forget to creosote the parts that go into the ground.

Log teepees are seen quite frequently and serve more as gathering places and shelters than as climbers. Still, they are nice to look at. If you predrill all the holes, you can string the assembly together like a necklace. If you extend the ridge pole you can hang a rope or tire swing from it.

LOG LADDER

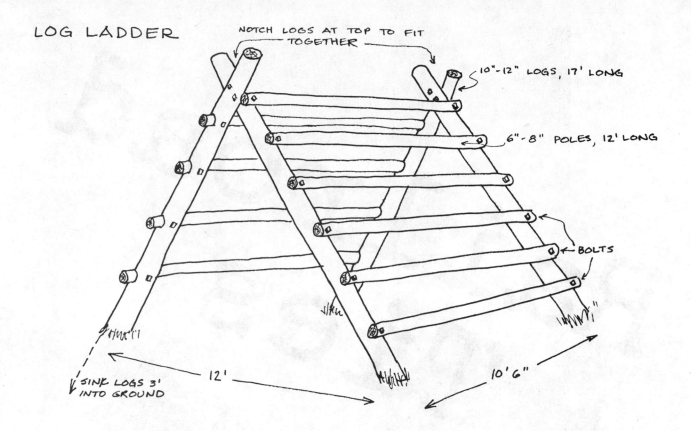

NOTCH LOGS AT TOP TO FIT TOGETHER

10"-12" LOGS, 17' LONG

6"-8" POLES, 12' LONG

BOLTS

SINK LOGS 3' INTO GROUND

12'

10' 6"

LOG TEEPEE

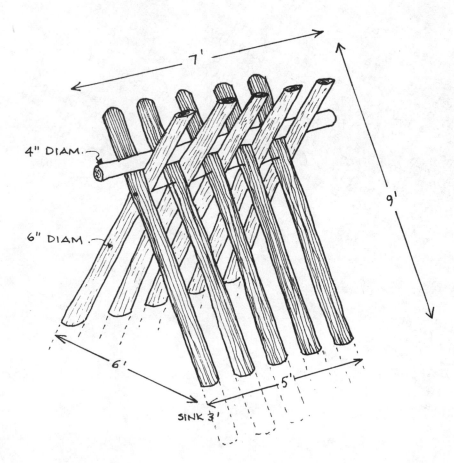

7'

9'

4" DIAM.

6" DIAM.

6'

5'

SINK 3'

Railroad Ties

As many as fifty children at a time can use this 60-foot slide at the Roberts' Elementary School in King of Prussia, Pa. The stainless steel is 22-gauge. This steel was purchased with funds from a cake sale. You must buy the steel at a steel supply house. The steel used here should have been heavier to resist the impacts of thousands of children who have bounced down the slide. Now I use 16-gauge sheet and eliminate the plywood base under the slide. Thus the slide can follow the contour of the slope. I use 1 1/2-inch polyvinyl chloride pipe and bolt it from the bottom with butterfly (toggle) bolts.

The slide was installed in two days, along with a swing assembly and the railroad tie stairs. More than fifty ties were used and the fathers did all the terracing and lugging up the hill. Two 1/2-inch water pipes were used on each tie to hold it in place, in a manner similar to that shown for walls on page 49.

I installed a rough railroad tie landing platform to prevent the usual gouging of the earth. Withing two days, the ties were so smooth and slippery that every child fell as he left the slide. A good solid piece of reinforced 1/2-inch thick rubber mat solved that problem and now the children hit the bottom, regain their feet, and run up for another trip.

Unless the Penn Central and the other railroads make an about-face by recycling their used ties, this may be the last set of steps built in Pennsylvania out of used ties.

Perhaps it is too late to even think about
using old railroad ties for anything. This
very basic material was once the mainstay of
the landscape and adventure playground
movement. Now they are just about all gone and
I'm not sure they will ever make a comeback.
The railroads in their mad dash for
self-destruction have adopted yet another
labor-saving abomination: the Universal
Super Railroad Tie Wrecker and Job Eliminator.
Its a gigantic pair of scissors which is
mounted on the last car of a work train. Rather
than slide the old ties out for recycling,
the railroads chew the ties into three
pieces and cast them aside.
If the railroads could invent a machine to pull
ties out in one piece as they have invented a
monster to insert the ties, it would be a real
boon. Actually, I don't see why the tie
pushing machine can't be put in reverse to be
used as a puller. No one at Penn Central seems
able to answer that question for me.

This railroad tie fort in Nashville uses ties and hewn timber. Some courses are left out for view ports.

This is how walls should be built. If you use bricks, your wall will need a foundation. If you use ties, it needs long pins to hold it together. "Dead men" must be anchored into the bank of earth every third course if the wall is to retain dirt.

HOW TO BUILD A WALL

THIS WALL WILL FALL DOWN

BECAUSE

- THERE IS NO FOUNDATION
- DIFFERENT MATERIALS ARE USED
- THE BRICKWORK IS NOT INTERLOCKING

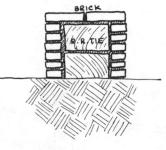

PROPERLY CONSTRUCTED WALLS

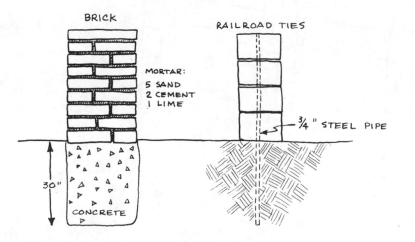

BRICK

MORTAR:
5 SAND
2 CEMENT
1 LIME

30"

CONCRETE

RAILROAD TIES

¾" STEEL PIPE

Orin Hogan is shown sitting out a work session in the early sixties in
Philadelphia. As shown in the accompanying drawings, the post ties should be
at least half-way into the ground every four feet. The horizontal ties should
be staggered so that the butt ends alternate with each successive layer or
course. While nothing much is left of the playground, the wall still stands,
as strong as the day it was put up.

RETAINING WALL

CROSS SECTION

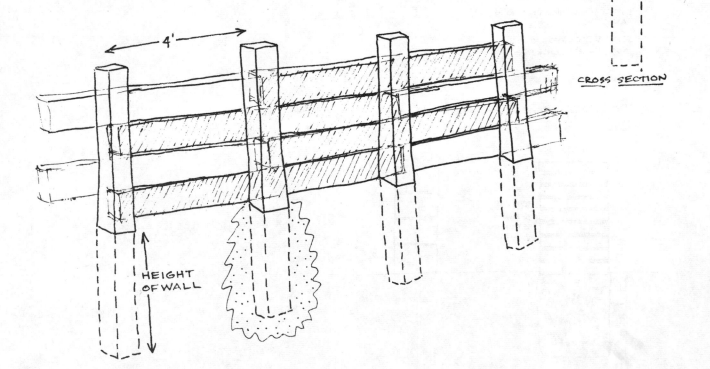

4'

HEIGHT OF WALL

I made these benches. The one on the left is constructed from one railroad tie and six utility pole cross arms. The arms are hard to come by as the utility workers usually take the used ones home for fence posts. I used 1/2 x 8-inch lag screws to hold the back on. For both benches, the ties were notched to hold the seats, and required no other connection. Make sure the creosote is well out of the wood before sitting down on it.

This sketch of an overhand walking/hanging device illustrates the basic design of many similar items. Such constructions can be made to go uphill or down; the hand bars, which may be made from wood dowels or steel pipes, can be spaced at different intervals. If you use a round utility pole for the beam, just notch the tops of the uprights and secure in the same manner.

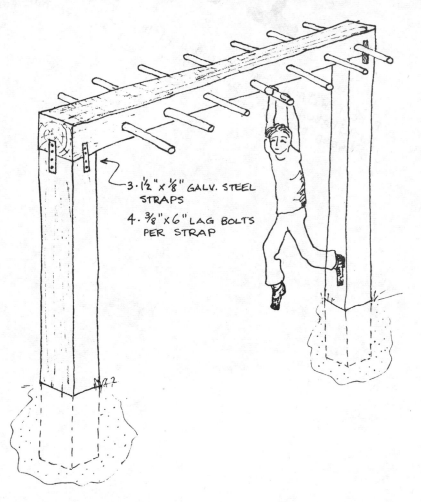

3 - 1½" x ⅛" GALV. STEEL STRAPS

4 - ⅜" x 6" LAG BOLTS PER STRAP

Tires

Robert Wilson comes through with flying colors on the tire wall built in a Washington, D.C., playground. The tires are hung from a heavy cable strung between two poles.

In the United States there must be at least
a half billion pieces of play equipment free
for the hauling. They are called tires. On
occasion I have been paid to haul tires away
and have made them into playground equipment.
In every one of the more than 40 countries I
have visited, tires were spilling over the
roadways into parks, streams, and every other
facet of our existence.

Emerson Sharpe is shown painting tires for the Professional Child Care Center
in Charlotte, N.C. This photo indicates how simply a construction can be made;
old rope and tires make a beautiful hammock. The paint used on the tires is
outdoor oil-base paint.

There are so many ways to use tires that
examples will be found throughout this book.
The famous Rokugo Tire Park in Ota-ku, Tokyo
(described in a later chapter), is made almost
entirely of used tires; and a fair business
enterprise (SWEAT Associates, described later
in this chapter) is built around toys made
from tires.

It is disheartening, but every time I publish
a new use for tires, I get three or four
requests from tire companies for information.
I have letters from four different departments
of one large company alone. I answer each
letter with specific suggestions for helping
to improve the environment by recycling tires.
I have never had a reply and I conclude that
the companies' only interest is in manufacturing
tires and making money. The environment is the
least of their worries.

A suspension bridge designed and built by Sam Vladimirsky, Director of the
Head Start Center in Ojai, Ventura County, Ca. Mr. Vladimirsky, born and
educated in Chile, is a registered architect as well as school director.

One simple way in which to help rid the
environment of tire pollution is to recycle
used tires into playground equipment!

If you live near Grand Coulee Dam or any big construction site, just ask the superintendent for a free tire. If you can convince him to show his boss that he can declare a tax write-off on the donated super tire, he may even deliver and plant it for you.

If you don't live near Grand Coulee Dam, any large off-the-road tire will do. In Newcastle, Bill Gohdes of the Pennsylvania Department of Community Affairs assists the children to construct a tire mountain at a local housing project. The teenagers were paid by the Pittsburgh Archdiocese Youth Employment Project.

EARTH MOVER TIRE

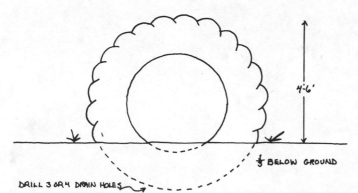

4'-6'

⅓ BELOW GROUND

DRILL 3 OR 4 DRAIN HOLES

This shows how to install a tire in the ground. Make sure that at least 1/3 of the tire is buried and that the buried portion is filled with rocks or tamped earth. Be sure to drill several drainage holes at the bottom.

1. Place large earthmover tire on top of good drainage area (stone, dirt, etc.)

2. Drill drain holes (3 or 4) in the bases of all tires to be used.

3. Drill 3 or 4 holes through tread of base tire and insert 5/8" x 6" gal. bolt with "D" head, washer and nut. To be used for steps, moving, and anchoring.

4. Place 2nd tire on top of base tire with 5" temporary spacers (wood, bricks, etc.)

5. Drill 6 holes at proper angle through 2nd and base tires as shown in plan.

6. Install 5/8" x 8" gal. bolts with large washers on top and bottom of both tires and 3/4 gal. steel pipe sleeve as spacers between the tires. Remove temporary 5" spacers and tighten nuts.

7. Repeat same method with each smaller tire.

8. Bolt wheelbarrow or scooter tire (or any very small tire) to auto tire wheel, as shown in photo, with 1/2" by 12" gal. steel threaded rods or bolts. Use 1/2" gal. steel pipe sleeves if desired.

9. Install steel auto wheel on top tire (automobile).

10. If trash inside tire tree will be a problem, place over a hoeing slot made from two railroad ties with a one foot opening for trash removal.

TIRE TREE

NUT

DRAIN HOLE

WASHERS

BOLT
SLEEVE

D-BOLT
WASHER
NUT

DRAIN HOLE

MATERIALS

24	5/8" x 8" gal. steel bolts
4	5/8" x 6" gal. steel bolts
4	1/2" x 12" gal. rods or bolts
100	large 5/8" gal. washers
28	5/8" nuts
24	3/4" x 4" gal. steel pipes
4	5/8" gal. "D" bolt heads
6	Tires, heavy to small

This, the original tire teepee, has spawned thousands of similar constructions. Each one is a little different than the other. Some are more elaborate and are ten feet high, and some, built for nursery schools, are only 2 or 3 feet high. The basic construction method, as illustrated, is universal with all such tire constructions.

Girl Scouts of La Cross, Wi., help paint a tire construction at the Harry Spence School.

In Gothenburg, Sweden, the children are bouncing along on a tire treadmill. Putting the tires in asphalt and anchoring them at a 45° angle improves the springiness of the device. This requires more effort and expense, but might be worth the trouble.

For variety of the tire walk, various size tires can be installed to form a tire mountain. For instance, we built a playground in a day with the Girl Scout troop from Haddon Township, N.J., at the Van sciver Elementary School. Not only did we see various size tires, but we alternated every other one. The results were very pleasing.

Judy Shatzoff is shown putting the Tiki god on top of a tire tree to ward off evil spirits and older kids. This was built with the help of Pennsylvania National Guardsmen, VISTA volunteers, and parents and children of the Serendipity Center in Honesdale, Pa. The original idea came from some friends of Northwest Design in Tacoma, Wa. Note how this construction is very nearly a totem pole as discussed on page 36.

This diagram shows the construction and installation of a tire tree. The pole should be at least 4 feet in the ground and the back fill should be well tamped. Rather than use just one bolt to hold each set of tires together, we now use two bolts with large washers. We found that using one bolt allowed the tire to spin; this was a potential hazard. Two bolts insure stability for climbing. Make sure you use big washers.

TIRE TREE

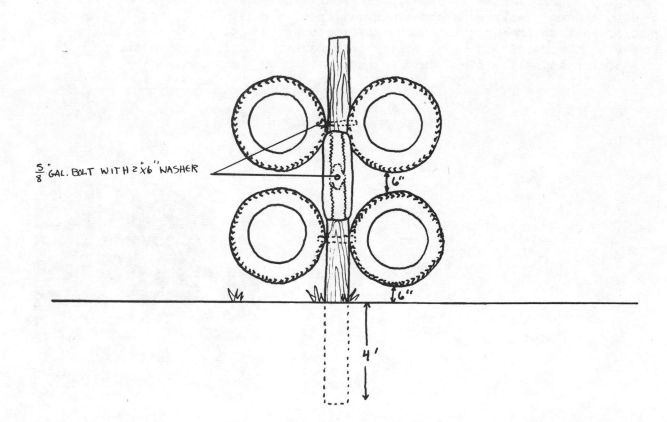

$\frac{5}{8}$ GAL. BOLT WITH 2 x 6" WASHER

6"

6"

4'

The Baltimore Department of Recreation and Parks designed this unique bird cage made of two large earth mover tires. Note the heavy chain used to support the assembly.

During my tour of Japan, I came upon a small elementary school in Sato. This tire toss game really puts the older children to work. The object of the game is to toss the greatest number of tires on the pole with the least number of throws. It is a lot easier to remove the tires because the pole is in a socket and slips right out for easy access to the tires.

It always helps to have a good tread on the huge off-the-road tires so that the children can climb up and down more easily. If you local tire supplier tries to give you a bald one, ask for side blow outs. You just bury the blown out part and the tire looks as good as new.

The children of the Enfield Elementary School in Ithaca, N.Y., enjoy this pyramid climber. I first saw one in Tokyo made with steel pipe, but this one was imagined by a young student and built by the parents.

Rear view of the climber. Note the steps up the back pole. Playground Clearing House has been installing these around Pennsylvania; we extend the back pole ten feet past the front so that we can hang a climbing rope or tire swing from it.

Sweat Associates

SWEAT is the upshot of a story of a group of people, who, tired of waiting for city hall to build a playground, decided to build one for themsleves. Jack Gleason helped organize some of the unemployed on Milwaukee's South Side. His crew found a debris-strewn lot which belonged to the city and promptly began to clean it up and build a playground.

For their honest and productive labor, the SWEAT workers billed the city $670.50. Then they planted another vacant lot in wheat and billed the Department of Agriculture $294.00.

Well, some of the local politicians thought all this was outrageous. The problem wasn't only the presentation of fair bills for services rendered; it was also the idea that citizens should get up and clean city lots and build playgrounds. "Stop," they said, "cease and desist, put everything back - get your ugly playthings off city land." Jack queried, "You mean you want all the trash, abandoned cars and other divers items of junk dumped back into the lot?" "Well, no," said the city leaders, councilmen, and ward leaders, "just get your play stuff off. We might build a playground there someday, and you are obstructing orderly development."

So Jack and his friends, finding their efforts unappreciated by the bureaucracy, went into private enterprise. They formed Tiretoys, Inc.; they have an eight-page catalog and their constructions from junk are selling like hotcakes. Their mobile tiretoy manufacturing plant has toured half a dozen Wisconsin cities. But, as Jack would be the first to admit, anything Tiretoys can sell, you can build. So go get some tires and bolt them together in a thousand different ways.

SWEAT Associates blocked off a street in South Milwaukee to demonstrate their tiretoys. Every week they come up with a new use for tires.

This tiremobile, designed by SWEAT, is an inventive way to recycle old tires.
SWEAT Park was the forerunner of a whole new tire toy enterprise in South
Milwaukee.

Inner Tubes

A slippery slide pool can be made easily enough. Just find a sloping lawn, a big sheet of plastic and some inner tubes to form a dam. Fill 'er up and start sliding. Joel and David Anderson built this novel pool in just a few minutes at their home in Grand Junction, Co.

There are a few hundred million inner tubes available this week at your neighborhood gas station. Just trot on down and they'll load you up for free.

We are just beginning to realize that tubes have their own place in playgrounds, schools, and libraries. They make great seats for story telling. They are very comfortable for preschoolers to nap in. They make sleds that can't hurt anyone.

While I was traveling on the trans-Siberian railroad, I saw people using inner tubes for shopping bags. They would cut out an 18-inch section out of a big truck-tire tube. By heat-welding the bottom shut and adding a

If there is one thing trucking companies like to do, it's to give away their old tires and tubes. They just don't know to whom they should be given. These Kentucky children have great sport rolling themselves down hills with an old truck inner tube.

George Washington looks on as Kevin Buck gives his daughter Caroline a start down the hill at Valley Forge State Park.

strap (also made of inner tube), they would have a substantial, waterproof bag.

I've never explored the lifting and other aerostatic properties of inner tubes. You could raise and lower platforms and weights by air pressure. You can pack fragile things in boxes by using inner tubes to give you a solid, yet soft, packing. You can carry water in them for camping trips. You can use them for bouncing, swinging, and rolling. You can tie a lot together for trampolines.

I even hear that some people use them for swimming toys, but that sounds farfetched.

This is the back yard of the Developmental Center for Autistic Children in Philadelphia. An inner tube can be a soft and quiet place for children and adults to relax, talk, or just think.

During a lull in a playground demonstration in Rittenhouse Square in Philadelphia, I brought out a dozen inner tubes. Within minutes the children devised more than a score of games. This youngster is seeing how far the tubes can be thrown.

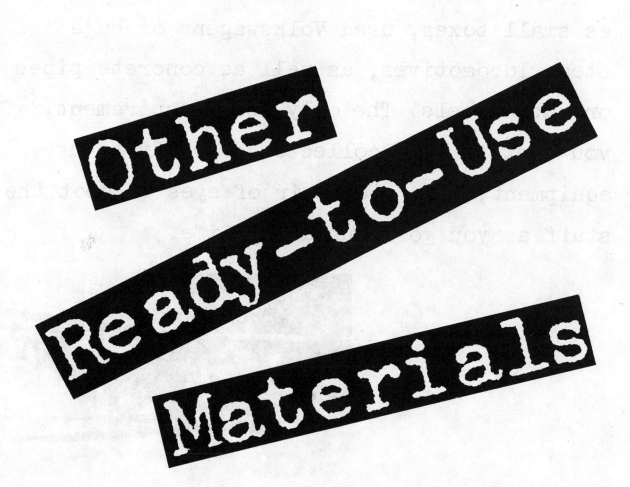

Blain Hibbard and Schell Foley sit on a tractor which has provided more than two generations of children great fun at the Charlestown Playhouse in Phoenixville, Pa.

Almost anything that can be hauled to the playground site and be put to use with little or no preparation falls into the "ready-to-use" category. It includes shipping crates as well as small boxes, used Volkswagens or huge steam locomotives, as well as concrete pipes or cable reels. The only real requirement, if you want to be a collector of ready-to-use equipment, is a good pair of eyes to spot the stuff as you go about daily life.

This single engine passenger plane donated by Central African Airways to the Amenities Department, Salisbury, Rhodesia, is a vast improvement over the jet fighter planes in American playgrounds. Recently, a jet fighter donated by the Air Force to a New York playground lasted only three weeks before the children set fire to it. Perhaps the children are trying to tell us something.

Ask the foreman of a construction job for his old giant tires and used plywood. He will be happy to help you and help himself solve a disposal problem at the same time. If you see a wrecking crew tearing down a building,

explain you mission and the wreckers will
most likely let you pick the place clean of
good useable lights, stairs, windows, doors,
and anything else they have to pay for just
to dump.

This old railroad car is in a playground in Vienna. There are few surplus rail
cars left in America. The make fine play shelters.

I spotted this caboose in a farmer's field while driving along the Indiana
Turnpike. The farmer's children have it all fixed up as a clubhouse. If you
are lucky, you will be able to find a railroad that will sell you a caboose
in fair condition and haul it to any point on its tracks for seven or eight
hundred dollars. But the supply of cabooses is dwindling and the price is
going up. At the Penn Central, there is a waiting list of 1,000 potential
buyers for cabooses that cost $1,000 each. If you have a good salesperson
in your organization, perhaps he or she can show the railroad the advantage
ot giving you a car free for tax and public relations benefits it can claim.
Getting the caboose from the track siding to your playsite is you problem.
They cost a few hundred dollars to have moved, but again, perhaps you can
talk a contractor who has a little time and equipment to spare to move it
for you.
Cabooses can be used for clubhouses, storage units, kitchens, lavatory
facilities, indoor playrooms, and just about anything else you'd use a
shelter for. They have stoves, bunks, tables, toilets, and all sorts of
other things built in and are great fun and very sturdy.

If you meet the people who are disposing of
stuff and can show them a newspaper article
about your project, chances are they will be
willing to get on the bandwagon by helping
you out.

I don't even know what this thing is, but the children at the Notting Hill
adventure playground, London, like it, and what else matters?

This funny-looking steam engine is in a playground in Durban, South Africa.
It was used at the turn of the century to haul sugar cane in from the fields
to the refinery. It still gives service to the children as a favorite
climber and plaything. How much better this is than a phoney simulated engine
made from cold steel piping!

I have a reputation in my neighborhood.
Whenever a friend sees some strange object
in his or her travels, he or she calls and
tells me, "Hey, I was driving down Route 29
and I saw this huge box with holes in it and
a pipe or something sticking out." I drop
what I'm doing and go look at the find. Often
the object is just cluttering the environment.
With a little help, a bucket of paint or some
plywood, it can be made into a useful play
object.

Bulldozer, motor launch, and oil truck are all in the playgrounds of Ota-ku,
Tokyo. Many aspects of Japanese daily life are represented and the children
naturally accept the play equipment with which they can most relate.

Don't be afraid to look around and get to know your neighborhood and let people know you are a "strange object" collector. People love to spot things and be recognized for the creative thought that leads to the recycling of throw-aways.

The boat has hit the beach and everyone is on the run at the Charlestown Playhouse. There must be a million boats that are free for the hauling. Look around, place an ad in the paper asking for boats or elephants. You'll get results.

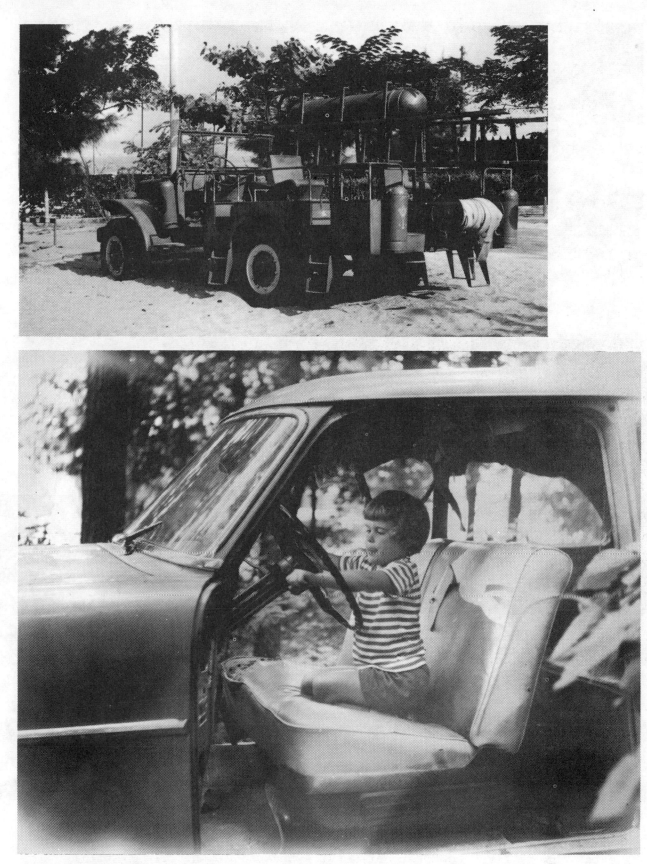

This surplus fire engine is in a Luanda, Angola, park.

Deedee Washburn tries her hand at the wheel of a Mark IV something or other car. They can be had for the asking, but take the doors off to prevent mashed fingers.

Tell your friendly neighborhood bowling alley operator that you'll have hordes of future bowlers for him if he just donates his old pins to your playground. The one in my neighborhood sells ten for a dollar to be used for firewood! If you can, make some wooden balls and reenact the ancient and honorable game of outdoor bowls. After they get splintered beyond use, they still make good firewood.

Art Fabian, a teacher at the Olive Hill Elementary School in Trotwood, Oh., obtained this Marine Locust tree from a roadway which was being enlarged. He expects four or five good years of service because of the tree's ability to withstand moisture, bugs, and ten kids at a time.

The Rapid Run Park in Cincinnati, Oh., has several old parachutes. These cost about $30.00 each, but can be a lot of fun. Just waft them up and watch them billow down.

Diane Stowell sent me this photo of the largest engine in Alaska. After the war, it worked for a score of years for the Alaskan Railroad. Now it rests in a park in Anchorage.

Alton, Il., has a whole playground full of engines and cars. Shown above is a boxcar being loaded onto a contractor's truck. The car was given to Alton by the Illinois Central Railroad; the contractor donated his work. The car, after it is repainted, will be used to store playground equipment.

On Picking Trash

Not too long ago, a decade or two before the junk society, vacant lots were
really vacant. Few people were rich or foolish enough to throw away a soda
bottle worth a nickle. A worn-out tire was always retreaded and precious few
were discarded. Shopping carts never left the supermarket to be deserted in
the gutters. Abandoned cars were beyond imagination.

My friends and I spent hours every Saturday morning cleaning empty lots of
such rare treasures as returnable soft drink bottles, scrap metal, and
newspapers, rags, and cardboard. More often than not our salvage efforts
bought our admission to the afternoon matinee. If pickings were really good
and we chose trash day in the right block, we made enough for the movie and
a candy bar besides.

Many of Phildadelphia's politicians and practically all of our lawyers must
have gotten their early training trying to convince the corner grocer that
their moms really did buy the soda in his store despite the dirt and grime
from a year's exposure in an undiscovered corner of a vacant house. We felt
the grocer had a moral duty to fork over the deposit and provide us with the
admission to another world populated by Dick Tracey, Killer Kane, and Tom
Mix. Except for one terrible period in history when someone - Mayor Wilson or
President Roosevelt - imposed a 1¢ amusement tax, the tickets were just a
dime - or five small Pepsi bottles, or a hundred pounds of old newspapers, or
a rusty steel wheel. Now the children's shows are rated X and all the Pepsi
bottles in creation wouldn't equal the price of a ticket.

On entering the Overbrook Theater or the Hamilton, each kid got a stub
numbered from one to ten. After the cartoons and before the Flash Gordon
serial, they showed a crazy race. Each week the same ten stooges, with their
number fore and aft, would participate in a contest of speed and idiocy. One
week they would have a wheeled race. Within seconds after the starter's gun
went off every vehicle would break down and the contestants would resort to
baby carriages, broken wagons, scooters, and wheelbarrows with square wheels.
The next week the race would be on water and they would use old bathtubs with
oars. Perhaps that's where I learned to appreciate the utilization of junk
materials: to make copies of the outlandish vehicles they used in the movies.
There was always a pretty maid or an outraged fat man in the tubs who were
unceremoniously dumped out for the sake of the race. They would use leaky
canoes, big buckets, barrels and anything that would, but usually didn't,
float. Bedlam reigned supreme during the fifteen minute marathon. And if
your number won, you dashed up to the stage to claim your prize candy bar,

and God help the manager if he didn't have enough to go around. The Ham is closed now and the Overbrook is a bakery.

When we weren't busy cleaning up vacant lots of valuables we occupied ourselves by walking along the gutters of our neighborhood looking for loot. We'd walk miles collecting cigarette butts, packages, and match books. We'd put our treasures into old school bags and take them to our clubhouse, the boiler room of a broken-down steam shovel. There we'd peel off the tinfoil and add it to the great balls constantly in the making. I don't remember if we ever sold those balls for scrap. I think the idea of selling 5,000 pieces of foil collected over a year and made into a thirty pound ball one foot in diameter for just two dollars was too much for us, despite the neverending need for money.

We poured the tobacco from the butts into a pile and rolled our own weeds in a hand-operated cigarette machine which sold for a dollar. It rolled perfect cigarettes and I imagine such devices are still being used by a younger generation but with different ingredients. Perhaps because our cigarettes were an unscientific blend of old stale Camels, Fatimas, and Lucky Strikes (before the green went to war), most of us gave up smoking before we reached fourteen.

We traded the book matches back and forth and some of the more persistent collectors had over 1,000 different books. We kept duplicates for future trading and used the paper and cellophane to light the campfires where we burnt potatoes.

Even now, in my forties, I like to pick trash. But it's no fun anymore. It's not because I'm getting old, it's just that trash is inferior nowadays. It's all plastic and low grade cardboard. The tinfoil is photographed onto the cigarette paper and you couldn't make a ball the size of a marble with ten million packs. There are precious few cedar cigar boxes. You could never hope to find the raw materials for a scooter. Today's orange crates are just pressed cardboard and the skates are blue and yellow plastic, not the steel ones we'd find that still had 100 miles on them.

Before the junk society, our streets were clean. It was for fun and profit that we weren't litterbugs. Everything had value: tires, bottles, wood scraps, papers, rags, cardboard boxes, and scrap metal. The plastic age, like the second glacial period, is now burying us alive. The ice melted over a span of many millenia; how many millenia will it take for a polyethylene milk carton to disolve?

2 Using the Materials

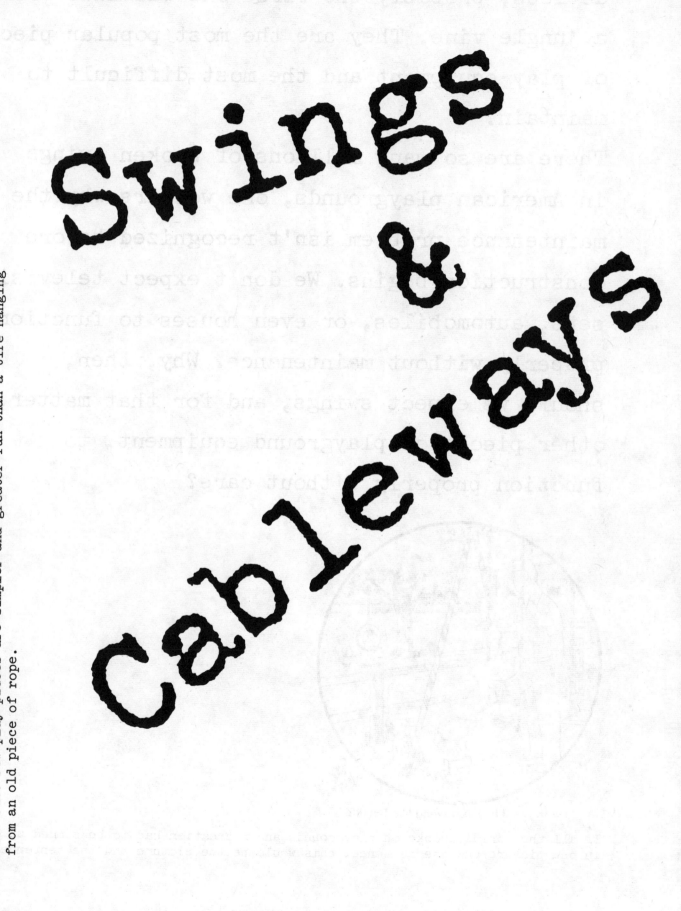

Swings & Cableways

The tire swing must have been invented about five minutes after the first blow-out. Few play pieces are simpler and greater fun than a tire hanging from an old piece of rope.

Swings may be one of the oldest of play devices; probably the first one was made from a jungle vine. They are the most popular pieces of play equipment and the most difficult to maintain.

There are so many millions of broken swings in American playgrounds, one wonders why the maintenance problem isn't recognized before construction begins. We don't expect television sets, automobiles, or even houses to function properly without maintenance. Why, then, should we expect swings, and for that matter, other pieces of playground equipment, to function properly without care?

"I wish you'd buy us a swing like THEIRS!"

If all the world's books on playgrounds and recreation had to be summed up in one picture and one sentence, this would be the picture and the sentence.

A swing can be anything from a gigantic tire supported by an elaborate chain arrangement to a rope looped over a tree limb. Swings can be two feet high for two-year olds or forty feet high for forty-year olds. They can be put up for an hour, or put up for ever, if taken care of properly. Many recreation departments and schools have solved the problem of maintaining swings by eliminating them. This denies the children a very important play activity and illustrates a typical head in the sand approach to play.

These examples of a new tire-swing design came to me from Tennessee and Kenya within a few weeks of each other. This design is especially useful for small children who haven't mastered the fine art of tire swinging.

The most important thing for a swing assembly is to first tear up the blacktop in playgrounds, where the majority of swings are constructed. The surface should then be replaced with dirt, sand, wood chips, sawdust, foam rubber scraps, or any other soft material which can be obtained for free. The playground staff must be prepared to constantly refill the groove created by thousands of swinging children. Large sections of heavy rubber conveyor belting can also be used. This material is over 1/2-inch thick and comes in pieces 3 or 4 feet wide. It can be nailed to railroad ties set flush in the ground, or directly to unremoveable asphalt.

Not all swings have to be tires. Any rope hanging from a tree or beam will do. Orin Hogan is shown boarding a rope swing piloted by Jimmy MacMichael in the author's back yard.

The Pacific Gas & Electric Company installed this flying unit in one of the
few adventure playgrounds in America. This is located at the Milpitas, Ca.,
Recreation/School District Playground. It builds up the arm muscles of
children while helping them to overcome the fear of height and motion.
The cargo net at the base station gives them a gentle stop and an opportunity
to clamber down safely.

The next most important thing is to be sure
that the swing supports are sturdy enough for
the wear expected of them. Wherever possible
for permanent swings, use 5/8-inch swivels and
clevis bolts, and 5/16-inch or larger chain.
Even so, I have found that the shackles on
heavily-used swings tend to wear out after about
three months. At the Playground Clearing House
we are attempting, with some success, to solve
this problem by using old truck steering-column
universal joints as swing suspensions.
So don't be an ostrich, look to the heavens and
hang that swing.

Here's a tiny tot version of the cantilever swing. The construction was
designed and built by Richard Graham of the Minneapolis College of Art and
Design. The lumber was salvaged from an old warehouse and treated with
Penetrol to keep down splinters. The mural in the background was painted by
Leorna Berman.

Swings and cableways don't have to be permanent installations. They can be
set up at fairs and temporary playgrounds.

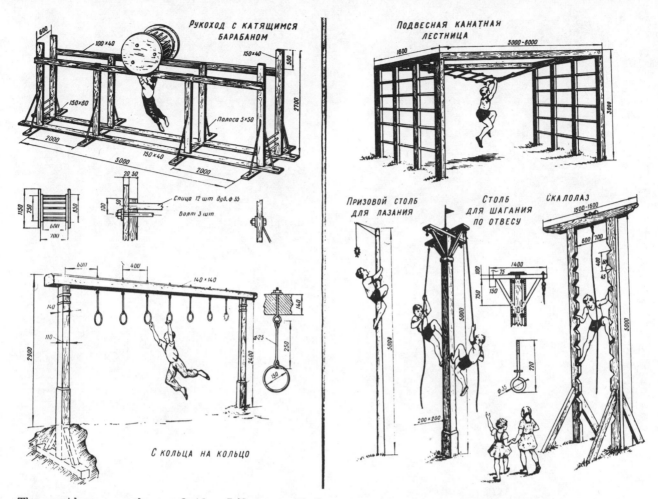

The nether reaches of the Library of Congress produced this excerpt from a Russian book on playground construction. Most of the equipment shown in the book is geared toward the development of the upper body areas.

Susan Hefferman demonstrates the latest use for an ATV (all terrain vehicle) tire. Jerry Frey, Superintendent of Vanango County's Two-Mile-Run Park, designed and installed this item. Just a big washer and a cable clamp was all that was needed to secure the tire to the cable.

A board placed between two tire swings provides a new thrill for the students of a school in Plainfield, N.J.

Teacher James Joyner of Lincoln, Ne., High, along with his shop students, designed and built this huge tire doughnut for the children of a nearby Day Care Center. It's like a huge waterbed. When one tire is moved, they all vibrate together.

Within a few days of receiving the photo from Nebraska, I received a similar one from Otto's Day Care Center in Kankakee, Il. The tires are bolted together to form a circle and are suspended from utility poles. Men from "Operation Mainstream" provided the labor and the whole project was sponsored by the Kankakee Community Action Program.

The most elaborate monkey swing I have ever seen is in the Traffic Park in Ota-ku, Tokyo.

A simple monkey swing can be built according to the plans shown here. Less permanent alternatives to the turnbuckles are long eyebolts with nuts which you can draw up taut after the cable is attached.

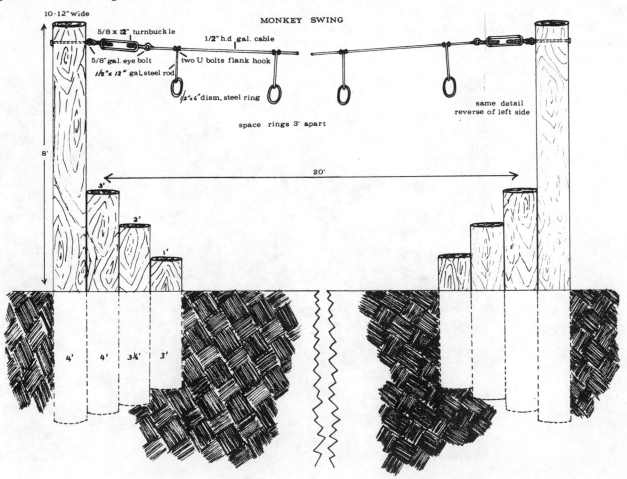

MONKEY SWING

10-12" wide

5/8 x 12" turnbuckle

1/2" h.d. gal. cable

5/8" gal. eye bolt

two U bolts flank hook

1/2" x 12" gal. steel rod

1/2" x 6" diam. steel ring

space rings 3' apart

same detail
reverse of left side

8'

3'

2'

1'

20'

4'   4'   3½'   3'

繩粗（直徑）約3公分，踏板離地約30公分。

材料：架子可用普通木料或鋼管做成，繩索 可 用純白麻絞成，繩上最好塗上一層防磨油類，以便延長使用時間。

3.浪木：浪木是鍛鍊兒童身體平衡的運動器材，有半圓、整圓和方形三種樣式。

尺寸：浪木兩端的木架好像門框，架高2公尺70公分，寬約1公尺60公分。浪木長約5公尺至6公尺50公分，粗（直徑）約15公分至20公分。

離地高約15公分至20公分，兩端必須留出4公尺的空地，以便浪木擺勁。

在浪木兩端各15公分範 圍內，裝一鐵環，用鐵索或麻製繩索懸掛架上。繩粗（直徑）約3公分至4公分，長2公尺50公分左右。兩繩上端相距較寬，以兒 童肩部能自由穿過爲宜。

材料：與鞦韆相同。

4.飛馬：飛馬

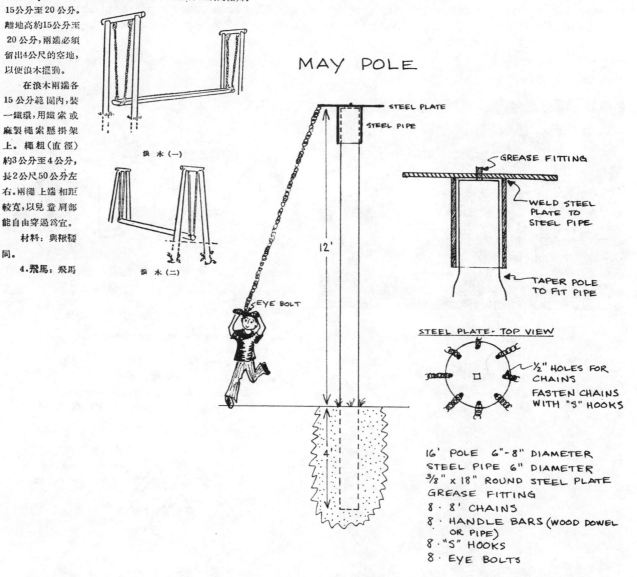

MAY POLE

STEEL PLATE
STEEL PIPE

GREASE FITTING

WELD STEEL PLATE TO STEEL PIPE

TAPER POLE TO FIT PIPE

12'

EYE BOLT

4'

STEEL PLATE · TOP VIEW

½" HOLES FOR CHAINS

FASTEN CHAINS WITH "S" HOOKS

16' POLE 6"-8" DIAMETER
STEEL PIPE 6" DIAMETER
3/8" x 18" ROUND STEEL PLATE
GREASE FITTING
8 · 8' CHAINS
8 · HANDLE BARS (WOOD DOWEL OR PIPE)
8 · "S" HOOKS
8 · EYE BOLTS

浪 木（一）

浪 木（二）

This wooden plank swing is excerpted from a Korean book on recreation equipment and is similar to the Plainfield, N.J., double tire swing (page 89). Perhaps some restraining chains should be put on it so the children don't fly off the handle.

This maypole can accomodate two to eight children as long as they are evenly balanced as they swing around in ever widening circles. A good ball bearing assembly is preferable to the grease fitting illustrated here. Strangely enough, ball bearing fittings are easily come by. The manufacturers work with such close and exact tolerances that they often have factory rejects which are completly worthless to industry, but invaluable for playground merry-go-rounds, maypoles, etc. For the Haddonfield, N.J., merry-go-round, SKF Industries donated a reject ball bearing assembly worth $150.00 that did a perfect job, and that the kids have been spinning around on now for more than a year.

The children of this school in Tanzania may not have access to regular utility poles or tires, but they make good use of bamboo poles which grow nearby. This inverted seesaw swing can be made with all sorts of sturdy, light poles. All you need is a tree to hang it from.

If you positively must have the conventional seat swing assembly, here's a design for one. Ask your utility company for the poles and the all-important pole hinges, as illustrated in the drawing. If these poles aren't set deep in the ground (four feet), you will need two more poles to form a tripod at each end to prevent racking.

This large size super seesaw swing was built by students for an elementary school in Grand Rapids, Mi.

THREE SWINGS

22'

10'

3'

1 · 22' POLE
4 · 16' POLES
3 · 6"x22" WEATHERPROOF BOARDS
CABLE OR ROPE
6 · EYE BOLTS 5/8"x12"
2 · BIPOD HINGE CONNECTORS
(AVAILABLE FROM UTILITY COMPANY)
2 · 4' PERFORATED STEEL STRAPS 3/16"x1½"

STEEL STRAP:
NAIL TO POLES

This version of the cantiliver tire swing was recently built at Stans Park in
Blue Island, Il. The hole needn't be as deep as indicated on page 35, due to
the two upright posts halfway up the swing pole.

Renee Haman is shown pushing some kids around on a cardboard tube swing. But
Blair McKinney, Christopher McGibbon, and Cappy Pilchard don't seem to mind
too much. Students from the Brooks Institute's School of Fine Arts, under
instructor Charles Latkoff, built the play equipment for the Montessori School
in Santa Barbara, Ca.

This cartoon has appeared in a half dozen magazines. Each gives credit to a different person. I hope its originator doesn't mind.

AS PROPOSED BY THE PROJECT SPONSOR

AS SPECIFIED IN THE PROJECT REQUEST

AS DESIGNED BY THE SENIOR ANALYST

AS PROGRAMMED BY THE PROGRAMMERS

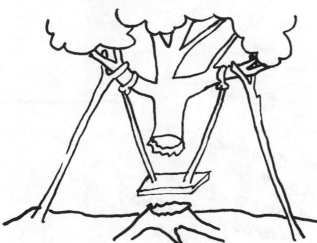

AS INSTALLED AT THE USER'S SITE

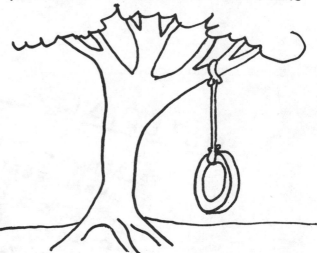

WHAT THE USER WANTED

Animals

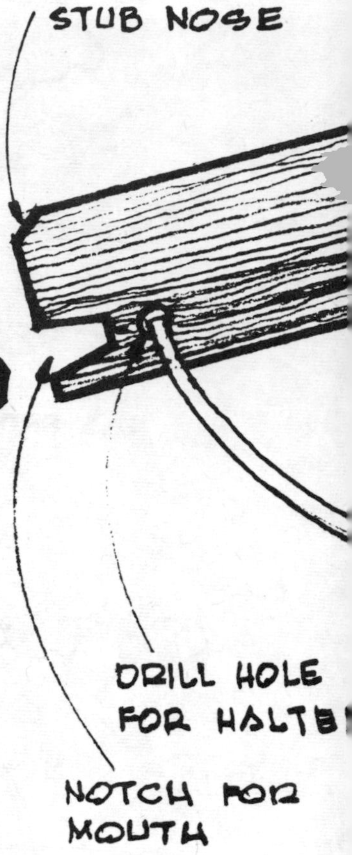

STUB NOSE

DRILL HOLE
FOR HALTER

NOTCH FOR
MOUTH

MATERIALS

TELEPHONE POLE 8" DIA. APPROX.
15 LINEAL FEET

1/2" DIA. O.D. PIPE CONNECTORS
3-PIECES, 16" LONG

EARS – (2) OLD RUBBER INTERTUBE

HALTER– ROPE (NYLON or HEMP)

EYES – (2) 2" DIA. CAR BUMPER
REFLECTORS

TAIL – (1) 3/8" × 4" LONG EYE LAG
SCREW + OLD FRAYED ROPE

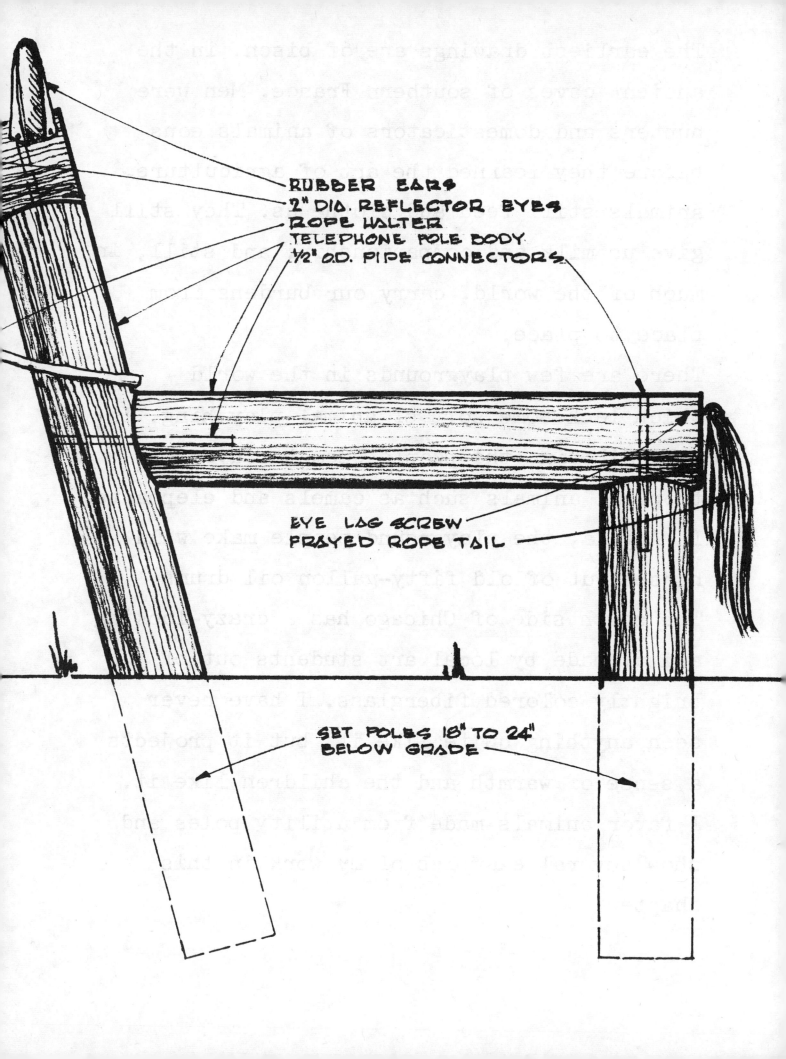

RUBBER EARS
2" DIA. REFLECTOR EYES
ROPE HALTER
TELEPHONE POLE BODY
½" O.D. PIPE CONNECTORS

EYE LAG SCREW
FRAYED ROPE TAIL

SET POLES 18" TO 24"
BELOW GRADE

The earliest drawings are of bison, in the ancient caves of southern France. Men were hunters and domesticators of animals eons before they learned the art of agriculture. Animals still feed and clothe us. They still give us milk and companionship, and still, in much of the world, carry our burdens from place to place.

There are few playgrounds in the world which lack some sort of animal plaything. In cold Siberia, the people seem to favor tropical animals such as camels and elephants. In Angola, the playground people make wild horses out of old fifty-gallon oil drums. The south side of Chicago has a crazy-looking animal made by local art students out of brightly colored fiberglass. I have never seen anything quite like it, but it projects a sense of warmth and the children like it. I favor animals made from utility poles and show several examples of my work in this chapter.

I bet you could make animals out of cable
reels, trash cans, railroad ties, or almost
anything you can pick up free. There are
exotic birds made from old reinforcing rods
in the underground mall of a huge shopping
center in Honolulu, and at a recreation
conference in Geneva I saw an exhibit of
weird birds and animals and humans as well,
made from tin cans. They were put together
by children at the Cologne Art Center.

This was the first utility pole horse I ever built. It was placed in
Philadelphia's Melon Park more than ten years ago. It was poorly designed and
didn't last long. The head fell off when ten kids tried to balance themselves
on it. The legs weren't firmly planted in the ground and the horse was soon
knocked over. I learned a lot from that horse, and subsequent ones designed
for wear have lasted for years.

So just gather your materials, let your imagination take care of itself, and out will come some exciting, playful animals. Whether you use concrete or utility poles, fiberglass or old oil drums, cast-off tires or funny-looking tree trunks, please make your own and help stamp out the concrete turtles that are endangering the playgrounds of the world.

Owen Hibbard, Lisa Nunnaly, and Cecilia Chang ride a utility pole horse at the Charlestown Playhouse.

By extending the pole horse's neck 4 or 5 feet, you have a giraffe. I use wooden insulator knobs to simulate horns. I also cut notches for steps in the legs.

This concrete alligator was designed and built by the author to show how the abominable production line concrete turtle can be defeated. Rather than spend three hundred dollars on a terrible tortoise, spend ten dollars on some steel rods, metal plasterer's lath, and and a few bags of concrete make any kind of animal you want.

The worst you can possible do will still be ten times better than the best the mass producers can crank out. Your turtle will have character and individuality. If you spend the money saved on a work/play leader, or artist, he or she can teach the children how to put the alligator together and they will learn carpentry, concrete, and sculptural skills, to say nothing of the pleasure of working together to build something worthwhile.

The artist/teacher/craftsman assembles the children and says, "Well, children, every playground or school has an animal and we are going to make our own concrete animal. What do you think it should be?" The immediate and unanimous reply is "turtle." The teacher shakes his head sadly and says, "No, no, children, the world is overpopulated with turtles already. Let's do something else." When the children start thinking, one will say "elephant," another "bear," "hippopotamus," "giraffe," whatever. Perhaps each child will come up with his own favorite animal and confusion will take over. The teacher comes back into the scene and says, "Whoa, there are so many wonderful ideas that we should have an election." Even for two-year olds, a democratic election can be held to choose the animal most wanted by the group. Let's say an alligator is chosen. The teacher then asks each child to draw his or her idea of an alligator. Each picture is signed and posted for all the school and playground to look at. Then the teacher takes the class to the library and shows the children how to look up alligators and shows them pictures and drawings and talks about the whole alligator world, their habitat, their ways, the fact that they are being pursued unmercifully by poachers, and what the government is doing to protect such endangered species. Children even learn about the alligator's cousin, the crocodile. Then, if possible, the children are taken to the zoo, where they see live alligators doing the things that alligators do. Then the class returns to the school or playground and the children begin planning to built their own alligator. First, they go to a construction site and ask the contractor for used or damaged reinforcing rods, metal lath, tie wire, etc. I've never seen a job yet without such material lying about and I've never run into a contractor who wouldn't donate these things for a good cause. Then, back at the school or playground with pictures and diagrams to support them, the children, with the help of

103

the teacher, assemble the skeleton of the alligator. They tie the metal lath on to support the skin and then they are ready for the next step. The teacher takes the children to the building supply yard where they buy a bag of cement, 200 pounds of sand, and some lime. Naturally, it would be much easier to use ready-mix, but that's not the point of this exercise. The sand and cement and lime are mixed together in a 6-1-2 ratio, the teacher explaining the properties and uses of each material. He shows the children why it is important to have the right amount of water mixed in; if the concrete is too wet, it slides off the form; and if it is too dry, it won't stick to itself. The children put on layer after layer over a period of weeks, keeping each layer damp so that it is cured properly and doesn't crack and flake off. In order to have a smooth final coat, sift the sand through window screening before mixing in concrete and lime. Any color can be added to the final layer; you can have a blue alligator or a green one or a pink one. The final coat is smoothed on with rubber gloves and kept damp for another week, and, finally, after a month of work and study and travel and investigation and planning, the alligator is finished.

For all intents and purposes, the alligator has fulfilled its destiny, that of pleasing the teacher and the children. The children have learned to think of something besides the turtle. They have participated in a real democratic election to choose their animal. They have learned something of library science, zoology, have been to the zoo, have learned some carpentry, sculpture, ironwork, and cement finishing. They have had a big slice of life taught to them in the most pleasing way imaginable.

What can a child possibly learn from a catalog-purchased concrete turtle?

I made a fiberglass mold of this alligator and made one copy from it. After that I threw away the mold. Two look-alike alligators are plenty for this world. One was donated to the Phonexville Day Care Center and the other to the Charlestown Playhouse, near Phoenixville, Pa.

Bernard Langlais, who lives near Freeport, Me., is a wood sculptor. This assemblage includes (on both sides) a cow, sheep, pigs, and dogs. The back of the animals form steps on which children can run up and down. How much better to spend tax money on this individual sculpture than on mass-produced animals having hard shells on top.

Gerry Golberg rides this ex-merry-go-round horse. This horse needs a lot of maintenance because the waterproof glue isn't so waterproof.

This horse and giraffe are in a little park in Shorewood, Wi.

Perhaps this wooden turtle will go forth and multiply and drive his million concrete cousins from the earth.

Max Fulton and Geoffrey Spinkle play cowboys on a horse while design instructor Charles Latkoff keeps a steady hand. This popeyed horse was made from cardboard tubes by students from the Brook Institute of Fine Arts in Santa Barbara, Ca.

Believe it or not, this concrete elephant slide in Khabarovsk in Eastern
Siberia, is pink! The children were in school when I visited the playground
but my guide told me the elephant is very popular.

The children of Khabarovsk in Eastern Siberia insisted that I photograph them
on their favorite camel. In the background you'll note that the terrible turtle
has invaded the Soviet Union on a production line basis, but the children
wisely ignore him. The camel was built by local park workmen and has an
individuality of character that no mass produced animal could ever achieve.

107

This bridge over a drainage ditch was built by VISTA volunteers working with the Playgrounds for Free program sponsored by the Pennsylvania Department of Community Affairs. The bridge leads from the Casey flood disaster trailer park in Wilkes-Barre, Pa. Used pallets, railroad ties, and utility poles were used for the bridge and now all the adults use it, as well as the kids.

Constructions

What are constructions? To me, they are the works of constructors, of people who build. A construction may be as simple as a seesaw, or it may end up being a total play environment. The important thing is that the stamp of its builders be upon it; and, more important even than that, that its builders <u>learn</u> from and <u>enjoy</u> the process of construction itself. Children need not only to be presented with playgrounds; they need to be invited to help build playgrounds.

These young race car drivers from Gothenburg, Sweden, have fashioned cars out of old baby-carriage wheels, boxes, and even an arm chair.

With a "nuts and bolts" grant of $100 from the America The Beautiful Fund, Richard Graham, of the Minneapolis College of Art and Design, built this cantilever climbing arch. It's on a vacant lot next to Dick's home. His students and neighborhood kids helped assemble the structure; it can support several dozen youngsters at a time.

I've traveled through more than forty
countries and lived in three. I've yet to
meet a child who wouldn't rather build his
own plaything than have others do it for him.
Yet we deny out children this right to begin
constructing their own lives in a medium they
can understand and cope with from an early age.
There are too few adventure playgrounds in this
world where the young are given the tools and
what little direction they need to build their
own environment from our cast-off junk.

In Vasteras, Sweden, the children play on a structure made from used lumber,
old tires, and lots of rope.

Students of Jim Joyner's carpentry class at Lincoln, Ne., High School particia
participated in meaningful work by constructing a playground for a local
day-care center. Here, simple shelters are shown being made from sheets of
plywood.

In this chapter's photographs of constructions
and the construction process, I try to show how
children and adults can work together to
build a play place and a play experience. It
doesn't much matter how the end result looks
or what the registered architects may think of
it. If the children are learning to live, what
can be more important than that?

You can spend weeks and hundreds of dollars designing and erecting a post
climber - or you can just get a pile of wood and bolt it together to please
the eye. The parents of the Central School in Haddonfield, N.J., and I built
this climber out of salt treated 6 x 6's and it came out perfectly. We did
lower the top rail when someone complained. The post climber was put together
in a little more than an hour. Notice the balance beams in the background - all
part of the maze.

On the West Coast, Robin Moore's students at the College of Environmental Design have provided these super building blocks. They are old bridge timbers and their sheer mass allows the children to built all sorts of things without using nails.

Warwick Estate, London, uses the cut-off slabs from discarded utility poles to create interesting constructions. Many utility companies have their own sawmills and recycle their old poles for blocking and cribbing. They will be quite happy to donate these otherwise useless cut-offs. You can make fences, house siding, bridge decking, etc., from them.

Art instructor Herb Limon of Wilkes College, Wilkes-Barre, Pa., sits on a catwalk. The structure was designed and built by his students for the playground at the Thomas Street flood disaster trailer park in Wilkes-Barre. The rubber is from old coal mine conveyer belting.

This play sculpture was fabricated from seconds 4" PVC (polyvinyl chloride) piping and connections. It was on display at the State Museum in Madison and then went to a playground. I've lost the name of the sculptor.

A cardboard tube suspension bridge supports Tommie Rowe and Max Fulton at the Montessori Center in Santa Barbara, Ca.

A New Jersey school had a lot of 4 x 4's and built this assembly. It would take more time to design this structure than to actually build it.

A granite curbstone finds reincarnation as a bench. This one is at the author's house in Pennsylvania, but curbstones may just as easily be put into playgrounds by the cities or the contractors that rip them out and store them in dumps. The dumps are full of them.

Land

scapes

While driving through a Pittsburgh park, I noticed this beautiful bench made from split logs.

After many years of general contracting, I
went into landscape contracting. There were
two main attractions for this change a dozen
or more years ago: the appeal of working with
less finished materials and the drive for
self-expression. In general contracting I always
had to follow someone else's plans and ideas.
In landscaping, I had a better opportunity to
inject myself and my ideas into the job.

Gerry Goldberg climbs a well-placed rock in the play yard of the Charlestown
Playhouse, Phoenixville, Pa. The rock was placed there to give a visual ending
to the limits of one grade from another. The parent helpers placed the smaller
rock beside the big one to keep it company.

There is a sort of Peter Principle for landscapers: "The job is designed to utilize the available materials, money and labor." To this day, my barn and land is filled with marble steps, railroad ties, old fountains, beautiful boulders, a nursery, and all sorts of other goodies which, someday, will find homes in other gardens. The main idea for a pack rat is to not throw any thing away, but find a use for it somewhere. That is pleasure.

This simple table on the author's patio was constructed of three sidewalk slates formerly set on Spring Garden Street in Philadelphia. I managed to salvage about 100 of these slates (note the patio itself), but the other 9,900 went to the city dump.

This simple bench is made from two pieces of utility pole with a piece of redwood set into notches. There are no nails or screws - friction alone holds the bench together.

This lovely old horse trough was snatched away from the jaws of a redevelopment
bulldozer and placed in a small park at a church in West Philadelphia. The
church elders wanted to help the community somehow. Karl Linn and I recommended
they take down the fence to a small neglected side yard and build a park.
Karl and I hired some neighborhood teenagers, who tore out the fence and laid
a nice herringbone brick pavement. Together we built benches, planted trees
and shrubs, and set the fountain in for the focal point.

Let that smart 3- or 4-year-old find his way through this maze, or find a place to hide from his little sister.

Space is left open (one foot or more) at the bottom of the walls so lost children can escape.

From an original design by W. L. Breti.

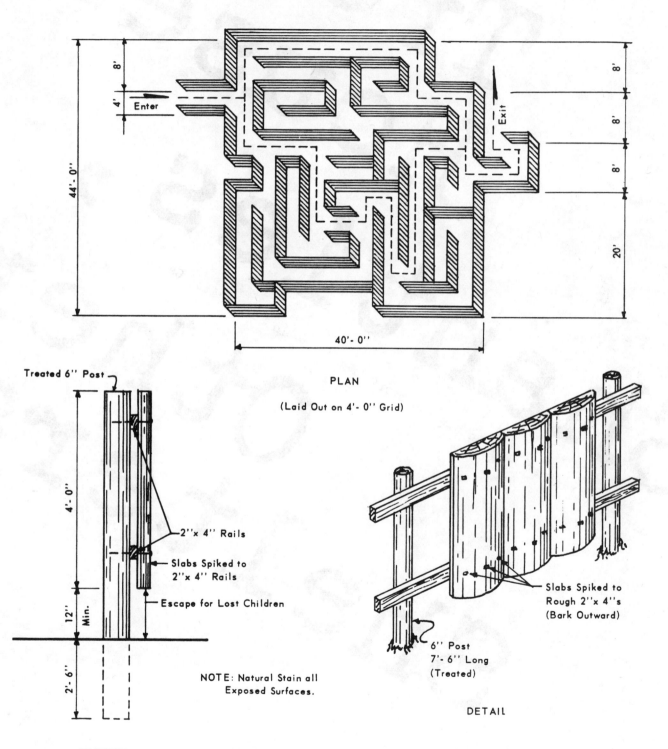

PLAN

(Laid Out on 4'-0'' Grid)

8'

4'

Enter

44'-0''

40'-0''

8'

8'

8'

20'

Exit

Treated 6'' Post

4'-0''

12'' Min.

2'-6''

2''x 4'' Rails

Slabs Spiked to 2''x 4'' Rails

Escape for Lost Children

NOTE: Natural Stain all Exposed Surfaces.

SECTION

Slabs Spiked to Rough 2''x 4''s (Bark Outward)

6'' Post 7'-6'' Long (Treated)

DETAIL

The detail of a maze and a fence made from pole trimmings.

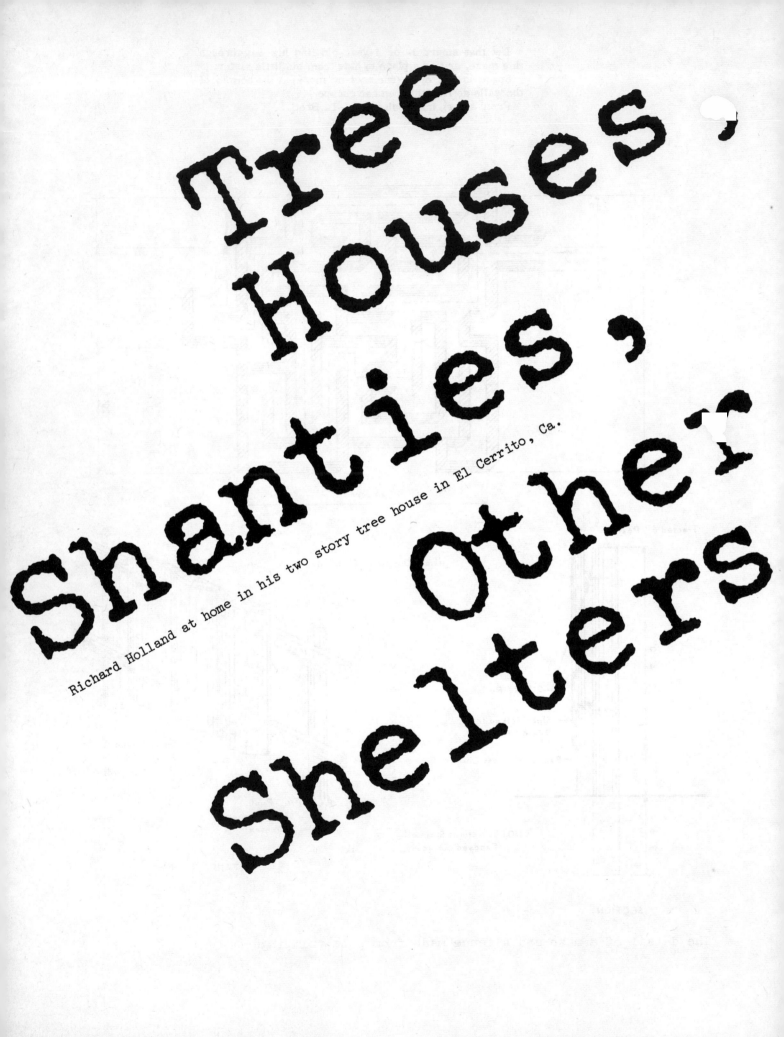

Tree Houses, Shanties, Other Shelters

Richard Holland at home in his two story tree house in El Cerrito, Ca.

I don't quite remember if the first tree house
I ever saw was in a Tarzan movie or in the
twenty-fifth century back yard of Phillip
Nolin, coauthor of the Buck Rodgers comic
strip. I know that it was more than forty years
ago that I played in the Nolin's yard. They had
a tree house which was, to my child's eye,
fantastic. In order to get to it one had to
climb another tree and take a cable car to
the house in the sky. I suppose that cable
extended only twenty feet or so, but it seemed
to me to be a mile long.

This tree house, which I and my children built, is more than twenty feet off
the ground, in a huge maple tree. Erica and Philip Sanders look out the
sliding windows which recess behind mahogony siding. The siding came from old
Yamaha Piano crates. Michael Sanders and Adrian Buck, near the trap door
exit, prepare to install an additional beam under the floor. The elevator
is made from an old cable reel, old rope, and a big farm pulley bought at
auction for ten cents. There is a plastic skylight and a small cabin stove
for heating and cooking. A good wind will made the cabin sway like a ship in
a moderate sea. Since this photo was taken, the children and I have added
a 200-foot-long cableway. Notice the heavy bolts in the branches to hold the
floor joists in place. They do almost no damage to the tree.

You had to pull yourself along the cable by hand while sitting in the basket. Once you got to the landing stage, you could cut yourself off from the rest of the world, and neither lions and tigers nor sisters and brothers could get at you. You were in a world of your own, your own Walden in the air.

I built this simple tree house more than a dozen years ago. The deck and railings have been replaced several times. The sliding board was made from a roof panel of a prefab building. When the slide gets rusty the kids slide down on wax paper a few times to make it glossy. The autumn nights are full of strange bonks as apples fall and hit the slide.

My own tree house was begun shortly after my first visit to the Nolins, and I'm still working on its descendents. The first was built in a willow tree in West Philadelphia. It had an elevator made out of a board rigged up on pulleys. There was a fire pole for quick exits, and I later installed a waxed-string and tin-can telephone system to my friend bobby Thompson's house.

Bobby's father was in the rug business and brought home lots of old packing crates from which Bobby and I made shacks two and three stories high. I like shacks and have built and lived in dozens of them; but my first love is still the tree house.

I saw this well-built tree house while driving through Lancaster County, Pa. I never went back to see who built it.

An inside view of Richard Holland's "Meditation Room." I've been to his two story house in the sky. It has stained glass windows, a fantastic bark paneling, a kitchen sink, and a bunk big enough for three.

Tree houses - particularly the more ambitious and successful ones - seem to evoke an extreme wrathfulness in building inspectors. For example, Richard Holland has a lovely tree house in his back yard in El Cerritos, California; I have included some photographs of Holland's house in this chapter. The town fathers have been trying to get Holland's place torn down for years; they have tried every ploy in and out of the books from "it doesn't have a concrete foundation" to "it violates the plumbing code." So Holland put a $25,000 price tag on the house and called it an "environmental sculpture." You can buy the house and the tree, but the moving costs are up to you. Meanwhile, the town fathers are busy drawing up new ordinances.

Tree houses, shacks, and shanties can be made from crates, cable reels, and almost anything else that has a top, bottom, and sides. With a little imagination, a saw and a hammer, you can make your own shelter in the air or on the ground. If you neighbors or zoning boards hassle you, just put a $25,000 price tag on it, call it "environmental sculpture" and wait for the buyers to stay away in droves.

Steve and Keith Haines proudly show off their two-story tree house near Bucksport, Me. They plan gradually to replace the burlap siding with wood. When I took this picture, they wanted to make sure that everyone knew that nobody helped them build their house. "We did it all by ourselves."

This triple-decker tree house is headquarters for the Empire Tree House Club of North Adams, Ma. Scott (Skip) Daniels, president of the club, is in striped pants on the top deck. Recently two more stories have been added to this house in a fifty-foot hemlock.

This geodesic dome was erected in just two hours by John Prenis of Germantown, Philadelphia, Pa. He put it up for the Fall Fooleries held in Rittenhouse Square in Philadelphia. He makes nice plan books which he sells for about 50¢.

Oskar Stonorov designed this habitat junio for the Charlestown Playhouse of Phoenixville, Pa. The fathers of the schoolchildren built it from old packing crates.

These two air houses were blown up in minutes by a window fan and a vacuum cleaner, respectively. They were featured at the Fall Fooleries in Philadelphia. The low one was constructed by the Synergy Network of Philadelphia and the high one was put together by the students of the Parkway Program of the Philadelphia School District. The plastic was obtained from a highway contractor who had no further use for the "curing plastic." Eash house was held together by a few rolls of masking tape. After being put up and taken down several times, the houses got pretty leaky so someone had to keep posted like the little boy ready to stick his thumb in the leaking dike. As soon as a hole was made by inquisitive fingers, the masker would run and tape it up.

Ken Morrow designed and built this "Mouse House" for the Fall Fooleries. It's made of just three sheets of plywood and can be erected and taken down in seconds.

Eddie Kimball, of Dayton, Oh., has built an igloo out of 40 orange cardboard triangles. The structure is five feet high and nine feet in diameter. Eddie scrounged the tape to hold his geodesic dome together from a local moving and storage firm. The interior is fitted out with a stereo set, TV, overhead lighting, and a plastic floor. It took three days to put together and weighs less than 100 pounds.

This scratchy old photo from the family album shows my daughter Paula standing in front of her private house. The door closer was a heavy bolt tied to a string. The photo was taken more than fifteen years ago and I don't remember if I ever got around to putting the roof on or not.

This bamboo Teahouse of the August Moon was built by children of the
Charlestown Day Camp, Phoenixville, Pa. It's a cool retreat from the rigors
of camp life.

This house in the trees was built more than fifty years ago in Oregon. In
another fifty years it will most likely be swallowed up by the trees growing
around and through it.

Carol McChonochie stands in front of a Philadelphia Fairmount guard house. The city often sells their old ones at public auction. I bought this one for $10. Do you know what your city is selling this week?

This elevated tire tower at the Lincoln Elementary School in Rocky Ford, Co., seems to be appreciated by the students. While this structure is made from new lumber, there's no reason why you can't build a similar one from surplus boards scrounged from construction sites.

At $160,000, this has to be the most expensive tree house ever built. Its first life as a liquid oxygen fuel tank for a rocket ship aborted after a truck driver put a dent in it. Sculptor G. C. Dwyer fixed the dent with a soft hammer and a block of ice. Then he put legs on the tank. Now, at the East Gate Trailer Park in Brighton, Co., it serves as a monument both to man's folly and to his ingenuity.

This log cabin took a whole year to build. The children of the Charlestown
Playhouse and I dragged the logs down from the woods. All of the logs were
dead and some were over thirty feet long, requiring twenty children to haul
them in to the building site. The roof is made of old sheets of concrete-form
wood with a scattering of second-hand plexiglass skylights. The three-year
olds laid a beautiful mosaic floor in just one morning; they had searched
the woods for the right stones.

3 How to Do It, How Not to How Not to Do It

The high point of Melon Commons just before the vandals took over. The marble amphitheater was built from steps salvaged from homes destroyed by urban renewal.

In the early sixties, Professor Karl Linn of
the University of Pennsylvania Department of
Landscape Architecture, Milton Shapp, then an
industrialist, and myself got "involved."
We formed a nonprofit corporation, the
Neighborhood Renewal Corps (NRC). The idea
was to help neighborhoods utilize tax
delinquent properties taken over by the city.
Our first and greatest efforts were devoted to
the Melon Commons site at 12th and Fairmount
Avenues in Philadelphia. Karl's students met
with the people of the neighborhood and
surveyed the site. Each student presented a
plan for the development of the Commons; the
winning plan was to have been selected by a
jury of architects and neighborhood residents.

The rooftops of Melon Park were a favorite hangout for the children. As the
children leapt from rooftop to rooftop, the town fathers criticized our
merry-go-round as being too dangerous.

A foundation had provided $12,000 to build one
playground. The students had to plan one within
that figure. All went way over the $12,000.
One elaborate dream had formwork alone that
cost more than $20,000. Finally a compromise
plan, incorporating the best of the students'
ideas, was adopted.

An "old head" looks over our handiwork.

Some children work and some play during the construction of the Melon
Commons. When this nurturing (construction) stopped, the body (playground)
began to die.

NRC borrowed a bulldozer, and we pushed all the rubble, junked cars, shopping carts, and car seats into a pile, covered it with dirt, and had the largest hill in central Philadelphia. Every weekend we brought in hordes of outside helpers. Church groups, fraternities, social clubs - all participated in building the playground. The neighborhood organization gave its token support and the small kids, at least, were eager to work. The teenagers hung around and watched. The city recreation officials came to offer suggestions, such as "You should level that hill and blacktop it."

Some local trash removal entrepreneur actually dumped truckloads of trash on our play sites knowing we'd haul them away. What an impact this had on the children.

Hundreds of "outside volunteers" worked in building the playgrounds of the Neighborhood Renewal Corps. It took some time for us to realize that people have to do for themselves to achieve success. One really can't hope to build a playground for someone else and expect it to remain viable.

Every day there would be some sort of mischief
played on the playground. Bricks would be
removed from our mosaic sidewalks, basketball
hoops would be knocked down, and trash would
pile up faster than we could shovel it away.
We made excuses. The hard fact was that there
was no neighborhood organization at all. It
was a paper group operating in a vacuum. At
the dedication, the mayor came, the police
and fireman's band came and played their tunes,
and the ladies responsible all received the
official certificates and orchids, but the
whole thing was a sham.

All sorts of volunteers helped. All had good intentions and we all failed.
The city destroyed this mosaic wall before the vandals had a chance.

The city officials were indifferent - perhaps,
in some cases, hostile; none of the people of
the neighborhood saw any reason why they should
work to nurture the playground; and every day,
as soon as NRC had finished its work, the site
fell deeper and deeper into disrepair.

Chris Speeth organized a children's theater and here are three young thespians
dressed as centurions before the marble steps of Rome. The marble came from
demolished houses, casualties of urban renewal. Soon after NRC left, the
steps - all three hundred of them - vanished. Where has all the marble gone?
Where have all the children gone?

One day Chris came out to my house and we built this 17-foot high Trojan
Horse out of plywood and fiberglass. The wheels were small cable reels. It was
a grand sight to see this contraption rolling down Fairmount Avenue for a
performance at Melon Amphitheater.
It was a joy to see twenty kids up in the box on the horse's back emoting their
lines and urging the 20 to 40 slaves to pull the tow rope faster.

We knocked this small plywood house together in a few hours and it was used in many plays at Melon Park.

Karl Linn (second from left) is helping to plant one of seventeen large maple trees donated by Hansen Brothers Nurseries. All but one was soon felled by one kid who had an ax and liked to use it. No one would stop him or say a word. I managed to save the last tree by wrapping it in barbed wire.

A mother stopped and asked why I was putting barbed wire on the tree. I replied, "This is war; I want the tree to live and the barbed wire is to cut up whoever tries to kill it." She gave a wan smile and said, "It's too bad, but I guess there's no other way."

The tree grew and flourished until the city destroyed the park.

The final picture of Melon. If you go to 12th and Fairmount, you can see this asphalt desert. It reminds me of Berlin just after the war. They rebuilt Berlin.

I'm including in this chapter excerpts from NRC's annual report for 1963, to show how some of our commons projects fared. Though NRC's projects were social and physical failures, they taught Karl, Milton, and me a lot. The lessons have enabled me to go on to build more than a hundred successful playgrounds. Karl has gone on to teach in Louisville, where he exhorts people to recycle; and I like to think that our experience with the real frustrations of living and attempting to build in our cities provided part of the motivation that led Milton to his present job as governor of Pennsylvania.

Neighborhoods That Can Help Themselves Can Be Helped:
From NRC's 1963 Report

The Horton Street project was most successful in every respect. The cooperation of the area residents was of the highest. There was money always available for needed purchases. The block organization was well developed and had a majority of the residents as active participants. The final phase of the original project was completed pretty much as imagined by the architect and residents. The marble wall in front and the railroad tie wall in back were completed with a minor amount of outside help. The seven locust trees have passed their first year with no damage whatsoever. Two seats were installed and the swing unit put up. There is the recurring problem with swing maintenance that is experienced by every playground where there is no permanent custodian to keep things in order.

The needs for this coming spring are a sliding board, ground cover and brick walks and patios. Several plans for a slide have been discussed and all require the investment of twenty or thirty dollars for the metalwork. Some bricks are now available but more should be made available after the first batch is down. While it is good to have a small stockpile of materials at the site, it is recommended that not too much material left around or breakage and litter will result.

The Horton Street operation was NRC's best project because of the stability and interest of the residents of the block. The geographical layout of the site contributed greatly to its success. The fact that the street was only one block long and was relatively isolated from the outside kept strangers away and litter and mischief to an absolute minimum. The site's being in the middle of the block also helped the whole idea. The high degree of home ownership on the block was an important factor in the success of this project.

If the Community's Not Ready, You're Not Ready:
From NRC's 1963 Report

The Pearl Street Project has limped along with very little involvement by
the residents of the area. Except for a few women leaders, one of whom was
paid, and one man, there was never any actual work performed by local
residents.

NRC made two basic mistakes at Pearl Street. One was in not properly
evaluating the community and the interest and ability of the people accurately.
The other was in the complicated original design and the numerous sebsequent
changes in the architectural plans. Unless there is concrete evidence the
community is going to back a project - unless a well attended neighborhood
meeting endorses it - the idea should not be carried any further by NRC.

Many factors about the site led to the failure of the commons. The proximity
to a public housing project where the residents are more transitory and have
no proprietary interest was the main reason for the lack of success. The site
was on a street with just a few houses and was situated at the end of the row
and across from garages. The street was too commercial and lacked the natural
presence of many residents who would be a check on vandalism.

...It is an unfortunate fact that those areas that most need the help are the
least prepared to cooperate with us and until such time as we may have a huge
budget and matching staff we have no choice but to stay away from projects
which don't evidence a high degree of cooperation and ability to follow thru
on a plan.

On only one occasion did a male adult go out with a group of teenagers to
obtain trees. Last spring a group came to my home and dug up a very large
maple tree over twenty feelt high. It was fairly obvious that the teenagers
were not enthusiastic about their volunteer job and I was of the opinion
that they were drafted into service against their will. This tree, along with
two donated by Sears Roebuck & Co., were planted by these same boys. Within
a week the two Sears trees were pulled out by the roots, and within a few
months the large tree died from never having had water and from general abuse
by the children of the area.

The lack of interest in the project by the local teenagers can best be
described by my inability of getting a few of them to help me hang a basketball net and backstop on top of a telephone pole which NRC and outside
volunteers had helped erect. Within a week after the net was hung, it was
completely destroyed. Everyone in the neighborhood pointed to someone else

or some other neighborhood as the guilty party, but the net was never replaced. The city donated several hundred dollars worth of topsoil and wood chips for the site but there were cries of dismay when the city was unable to do the final placing and grading. When it was pointed out that the residents of Horton Street were happy to provide the labor for the placing of similar loads of topsoil donated by the city for that project, a self-appointed leader still demanded and got more city help to place this topsoil. Even with the help of some of the Youth Conservation Corps crews, the project was never completed. One month later, the women called me and informed me that the block organization had agreed to pay a group of local teenagers $140.00 to move this topsoil and asked me to supervise the work. I agreed to this program and offered my tools for the work involved. I brought the tools on the morning of the work project, I was met by the one adult male who had helped me in the past. The boys had not shown up by the time I left an hour later. On returning later in the afternoon, the boys had shown up but a minimum of work had been performed. The fact that they showed up at all was important. I feel that to ask these boys to work for nothing is impossible and it is preferable to have them work for money raised by fairs or other community endeavors. The need for supervision of these boys is something which NRC cannot now provide. It would have to come from other quarters. The need for money for work performed is also very necessary in my estimation....

...This same community leader has called me many times on various complaints that we were not doing enough and were not getting properly involved. She constantly asked me for more volunteers from outside sources. I have consistently refused to bring in outsiders and I have tried to explain to her the futility of this method. She seemed to resent it when I told her that not only could I not get the neighborhood boys to hang the basketball net, but that they tore the net down after it was erected by outsiders.

There is very little remaining work to be done on the Pearl Street lot. A few hours labor by a half dozen serious workers could finish the project to a point where it would be clean and respectable looking even without trees or walks or other attributes. But unless this work comes from the residents, it is hopeless to try to clean up Pearl Street....

If the People Aren't With You,
They're Most Likely Against You:
From NRC's 1963 Report

...The manner in which NRC handled the Melon program was woefully ignorant of
the existing conditions. Without absolute support from a stable neighborhood
group, and a clearcut commitment from the city, working in an area such as
Melon is a waste of time, energy, and money, and does more to demoralize the
people than to help them. While the opinions of the local matriarchs should
certainly be considered, I feel that the views of the gang leaders and the
"old heads" who seem to head the power structures in each neighborhood are
far more important. Street gangs can make or break a project; and so far at
Melon we have been unable to penetrate these groups so that they will even
think in a positive way about our ideas and goals....We would install several
hundred bricks in a large patio one day only to have it ripped up the next.
It is interesting to note that only the bricks we laid that one day would
be taken out. We could put them back the following week and again the same
bricks would be uprooted - no more and no less than those we installed on
that particular day. It seems obvious therefore that the mischief was
directed more at NRC that at the brick patio itself.
The most important things to be recognized are the transitory nature of the
people and the absolute need for a program that has a plan spanning several
years. Further, it is unrealisitc to expect the people to come out in droves
to work for nothing. Until such time as the people can be brought to a level
of appreciation of a commons project, the commons sites should be as simple
as possible. This eliminates walls, walks, fancy benches, swings, seesaws, and
anything else that moves or can wear out or get broken. I believe that only
earth mounds, massive boulders brought in from construction projects nearby,
and imbedded telephone poles similar to those still in use at Melon Park are
the answer at this time. The only trees that are in decent condition at Melon
are those which were solidly wrapped in barbed wire....

The Lesson of NRC: From the 1963 Report

...What one thing did we learn out of this tremendous effort and expenditure of manpower, money and time? Local participation. That phrase is the key - whether the playground is to be in the ghetto or in suburbia, it all comes out the same. If the kids and their neighbors want a playground enough and are willing to build it together, it will work; if they don't work, the playground won't work.

Playground Clearing House, Inc.

For more than a half dozen years, I have promoted the idea behind Playground Clearing House. Few listened. Arvid Bengtsson, in his book Adventure Playgrounds (Praeger, 1972), printed my plans for collecting, distributing, and utilizing used materials for playground construction. Could not a staff of playground innovators go about showing community after community how to build playgrounds for free?

Recently, this dream has been realized. I recently formed a nonprofit corporation, Playground Clearing House, Inc., and the Clearing House has won several contracts from DCA. VISTA volunteers, who heretofore had worked for nothing, now can be paid to go into the various communities to assist in the building of playgrounds. Playground Clearing House now works out of Phoenixville and Lock Haven, Pa. It's a small but good start.

While all around us prices go up, and people become further alienated each day, the Clearing House staff feels that its program can bring costs down to near zero, bring communities together, and improve the environment.

Department of Community Affairs

This 20-foot slide at Oak Terrace in West Chester, Pa., was built from one piece of 18-gauge stainless steel, 4 x 10 feet. The DCA workers had it cut in half with a big shear. The rail is 1 1/2-inch PVC pipe toggle bolted to the 3/4-inch plywood base.

For more years than I care to remember, I took my ideas from city hall to city hall and from state house to state house. I carried a briefcase of plans, ideas, photos, budgets, and all the dreams I had developed over a dozen years.

Many officials saw me and heard me out. One high-ranking person spent an entire day listening to me and encouraging me. I left with him my most important plans. After I left his office I had mixed feelings. I was elated that someone was at last listening to me; yet I had a foreboding that I had been bilked, fleeced of my ideas. My feeling was confirmed a week or so later when I got my material back accompanied with a rejection slip. I noted, however, that the staples holding my dreams together had been taken off, my plans xeroxed and put back together.

This hanging rope swing is part of the obstacle course I built at the Paoli, Pa., Elementary School. What do you do when 200 children pour out of class for a 15-minute recess and there are only 6 swings? You built a junior size obstacle course. This playground cost the school $25.00. At the time this project was under way, a few miles down the Main Line another elementary school completed a contracted playground. Cost? $25,000.

To show the taxpayers of Pennsylvania how to build a "playground for free,"
DCA put on a demonstration of the program on the back lawn of the Capitol
in Harrisburg.
I brought 75 Phoenixville children, mixed them up with 75 from a Harrisburg
school, invited Governor Milton J. Shapp, and had a party.

William H. Wilcox, Secretary of the Pennsylvania Department of Community
Affairs, tries his skill on the cable reel log roller at the Playground For
Free demonstration.

This young lad flies through the air on the playground DCA built in a day in
Clearfield, Pa. The pulley is high-tension insulator. Notice the tires on the
pole. They make a very good shock absorber.

When Milton Shapp became governor of
Pennsylvania, I wrote and reminded him of
our mutual ideas about playgrounds. He
introduced me to William H. Wilcox, the newly
appointed Secretary of the Department of
Community Affairs (DCA).
Bill Wilcox asked me to present my ideas to
his staff. The wheels of government grind
slowly, expecially when you are waiting to
embark on a grand scheme. After several
months of negotiating and planning, we worked
out a small contract for me to provide technical
assistance to communities who had the will,
but not the money, to build their own playgrounds.
The first few months of work under the contract
were slow and disappointing. DCA's man in Erie,
Bill Gohdes, finally called. He had set up a
series of meetings for me. I flew out to the
northwest part of the state and met officials
and residents of a half dozen communities. We
talked and planned and a month later I went
out again and built two playgrounds in two
days.

I felt I had arrived. For the first time I was completely backed by a government organization. In the first year and a half after those first playgrounds were built in New Castle and Sharon, I, under the aegis of DCA, have shown the people of 120 communities how to build their own playgrounds. The cost to the Commonwealth has averaged less than $500 per playground, and the cost to the communities has averaged less than $50 each.

These children, living in a trailer park for flood victims of Hurricane Agnes in the Wyoming Valley, are celebrating midsummer's eve with the ancient and ritualistic Tire Dance.

DCA funded a recreation program for victims of Hurricane Agnes. Here, children are playing musical chairs around a tire teepee.

The most important part of the whole program
is getting people, young and old, to see
their needs and help them embark on
community efforts to build their _own_ playgrounds.
Without the enthusiastic endorsement of DCA,
these ideas and works would be light years away
from acceptance; the children of Pennsylvania
would be up to their ears in concrete turtles;
and their teachers would still be in thrall
to the playground equipment manufacturers
and their four-color catalogs filled with
$10,000 simulated space ships, plastic horses
on springs, and similar horrors.

Wherever possible, DCA tries to have music at its playground projects. I
think that perhaps the best piece of commercial play equipment is a public
address system.

Soon after Hurricane Agnes hit Pennsylvania, Secretary Wilcox asked me to go up to Wilkes-Barre and build playgrounds for the score of emergency housing villages set up in trailer parks.

The first thing I did was take an inventory of the materials available. I soon found this shut-down coal mine. The owner was happy to give me any or all of the equipment.

I took the mine cars to four trailer parks and the park managers threw me out with phrases such as "Don't dump your trash here." Finally one accepted and I got busy with free flood damaged paint, VISTA volunteers, and the children of the parks.

We built the Carolina Choo Choo (names after the park, not the state). The engine was an old 250-gallon oil tank, the wheels were from cable reels, and the cab was made from free boxcar dunnage. (Dunnage is the cheap wood used to brace objects inside freight cars to prevent shifting.)
After this photo was taken, we added a bell, the children have painted the loco a dozen times, and we even added a 100-yard station platform made from a 4-foot-wide coal conveyor belt. The rubber belt also serves as a cushion in the event anyone falls off the train.

People's Parks

The ultimate in playgrounds, to me, are
people's parks - play places built and
maintained by the <u>people</u> of a community,
rather than by some distant city hall. They are
also the most difficult to describe, build,
or operate. They are needed and are important
for the development of community spirit.

When I'm asked to participate in the planning
or building of people's parks, I do so with
extra caution. I'll talk anywhere and show
my slides, but I warn the groups of the
perils and pitfalls of going it alone. In
my talks, I place emphasis on organization,
money, and maintenance, rather than on a
spectacular work day to show up the devils in
city hall.

The devils in city hall are often quite content
to sit back and watch the park fall apart from
lack of follow-through. They know their posts
will be more secure than ever when a people's
park falls on its face.

The name "people's park" was first used, as
far as I know, by the young people of Berkeley
in 1969. This is what they called their park,
which was a great success. So the National
Guard was called out, and the soldiers came
and knocked it down. After all these years,
I still wonder why.

If the community still wants my services after
hearing my preachments of gloom and doom, I
insist on being paid. If the group isn't able
to raise fifty dollars for a token fee, they
certainly won't be able to maintain the site
for more than a few euphoric weeks after
"Work Day." Then the vandals move in with
their crowbars and spray paint.

If the people's park had one or two people who could hang in there and organize permanent committees, they would have a chance to survive. Who is the person designated to call the SPCA to report a dead cat or dog left on the lot? Who will see to it that the swing connections are examined and replaced? It's difficult enough to get a paid city maintenance man to fix swings in city parks. It's almost impossible to get any but the most devoted volunteer to do such work.

A People's Parks Committee should first have a fundraising gala before construction starts. Photos of other playgrounds should be displayed. There should be music and discussion and perhaps a big chicken dinner. The chicken dinner is perhaps a gimmick, but it does bring people together, it does raise money, and it does work.

Daniel McNeill came up to Philadelphia from North Carolina a long time ago.
He had to retire due to asthma attacks. Sitting around home he watched the
children tearing down the property in his neighborhood. When they weren't
knocking out the windows in the day, they were roaming the streets at night.
McNeill cleaned up a vacant city lot, and started to build a playground.
His slides are high, his seesaws wide, and his imagination without limits.
When I visited his playground at 1800 North Sheridan Street, McNeill was
resting and watching the children play. You'd have to see the half dozen
children spinning around in a commercial clothes wringer to believe it. He
set the spin baskets on a ball bearing base, three children climb inside and
others spin them into a blur.
The children and teenagers help him built the playground; together they paint
it bright colors. While the rest of the neighborhood is covered with trash,
McNeill's playground is an oasis of happy, laughing children. Everything is
built out of used materials. McNeill told me the children have kept him
alive these past dozen years.

Adventure Playgrounds

The world's first adventure playground, established in 1947 by the residents of a cooperative housing project on the outskirts of Copenhagen.

Adventure playgrounds are my idea of Nirvana. Those in the United States could be counted on one hand.

If you can't locate a surplus cargo net, do as the children in London's Notting Hill adventure playground did; make your own.

Robert F. McGuire, Director of Recreation, City-School Recreation Department, Milpitas, California, has created one. (The fact that Milpitas is progressive enough to join their city and school recreation programs is a great leap forward in itself. Why we have duplicate playground systems in this country is something I can't fathom. I see so many school playgrounds locked up tight after school hours. This is a social and financial luxury we cannot possibly afford).

New York City had at least a temporary
adventure playground when Gordon Mackenzie,
with a grant from the Astor Foundation, took
over the land where the old Ruppert Brewery
stood. The land, consisting of several acres
in Manhattan, was to be vacant for several
years prior to redevelopment.

Robert McGuire helped get the Milpitas, Ca., adventure playground moving. It's
one of the first in the United States to last more than a year.

Girls work and build alongside the boys at Milpitas. Too often we fail to
realize that women and girls gave a right to hammer nails and dig ditches
as much as men and boys.

MacKenzie brought in several hundred loads of topsoil and scores of people planted their own protected gardens. Other space was set aside for building and play and all sorts of recreational uses. I don't know how "the Greening of Ruppert," as it was called, has fared; but I hope that the land it's on will never be redeveloped, so that it can remain as a vegetable garden and playground on that crowded island.

This helicopter in the adventure playground at Ballerup, Denmark, has the latest grill and bumper from an old car.

Robin Moore and Clare C. Cooper, of the College of Environmental Design at Berkeley, have promoted Adventure Playgrounds in Boston and Berkeley.

This adventure playground at the Haag, Holland, is placed between a housing project and a highway. It is a buffer between the quiet in the homes and the noise of the expressway. A good use of land.
The children formed their own government and have a fire department, police force, medical staff, mayor, and council. The only time the adults enter the picture is to restore order if matters get out of hand and to help and advise on construction techniques.

Lady Allen of Hurtwood is beyond doubt the world leader in the Adventure Playground movement. Although Dr. Sorenson of Denmark should be given credit for developing the first one in the early forties, it was Lady Allen who took up the work of promoting this concept in England on a grand scale. I cannot

173

recommend too highly Lady Allen's book, Planning for Play (MIT Press, 1968), as well as Arvid Bengtsson's Adventure Playgrounds (Praeger, 1972). These two books not only describe the theory, but evoke the spirit behind adventure playgrounds. Those wishing to acquaint themselves with the work of an American advocate of adventure playgrounds should read Simon Nicholson's "The Theory of Loose Parts" (Landscape Architecture, October 1971.

The children's amphitheater at the Ballerup playground is made up of old boxes. The children write, produce, and act in their own dramas.

My dream is to help start an adventure playground movement in America. This book is a few steps toward the realization of this dream.

These young Austrian frontiersmen have built their own log cabin at the Kinderspielplatz (Children's Play Place) in Vienna.

No, this isn't a famous old Russian church. It is just a super shanty built by the children of Gothenberg, Sweden. The young carpenters and mechanics obtained the lumber and other materials from local businessmen.

Few American playgrounds are secure enough to support an old wreck of a car like this. But old autos are free and children can put them to good use. This adventure playground is at the Gladsaxe Commune, Copenhagen.

It's always good public relations to have a fence around an adventure playground, such as this one at Morrisania, N.Y.

I wouldn't want to stand lookout duty in the crow's nest, but everything else looks shipshape in this boat built by children (helped by adults) at Ballerup.

The children were off to school when this photo of their version of
Paddington Castle was taken in London. The playleaders helped the children
with this perfect stage setting.

Robin Moore helped develop this adventure playground in Boston. After the summer
program was over, funds ran out. The playground, without a fence or maintenance,
fell apart and another dream was shattered.

Robin Moore moved to the West Coast and now teaches at the College for Environmental Design at Berkeley. But he's still building bigger and better playgrounds. Here he puts huge sonotubes to use. These heavy-duty cardboard tubes are meant to be filled with concrete for bridge columns. If you fiberglass them, they'll last a long, long time.

Robin knows what to do with old washing machine cartons. You make a long dragon and have a party. Or else you can have a party and then make a dragon. Such cartons may be made into houses, elephants, steps, and a thousand other useful, if temporary, playthings.

A young parachutist in a West Coast adventure playground. I don't have a photo of his landing techniques, but he looks great airborne.

The older children of the Notting Hill playground built this structure for the five-year-olds.

The mud playground created by Robin Moore. I doubt if there is another sponsored site like this in America.

At a seminar on adventure playgrounds held in New York City, I met several people from the City College School of Architecture who had built the 118th St. Playlot in East Harlem. Though the lot was not really a people's park or an adventure playground, it was a great success as long as people were there to supervise play, construction, and maintenance. When summer was over, and the students went back to school, the playground, lacking this most vital attention, withered and died. How little it would have cost to keep the place going! Anyway, the City College plan reproduced here for a people's park is good and can be used if you want to organize a playground for you community. Like a human organism, a playground has to be loved and fed and kept alive with nutrients, hammer and saws, hammerers and sawyers, materials and children, lessons and adults.

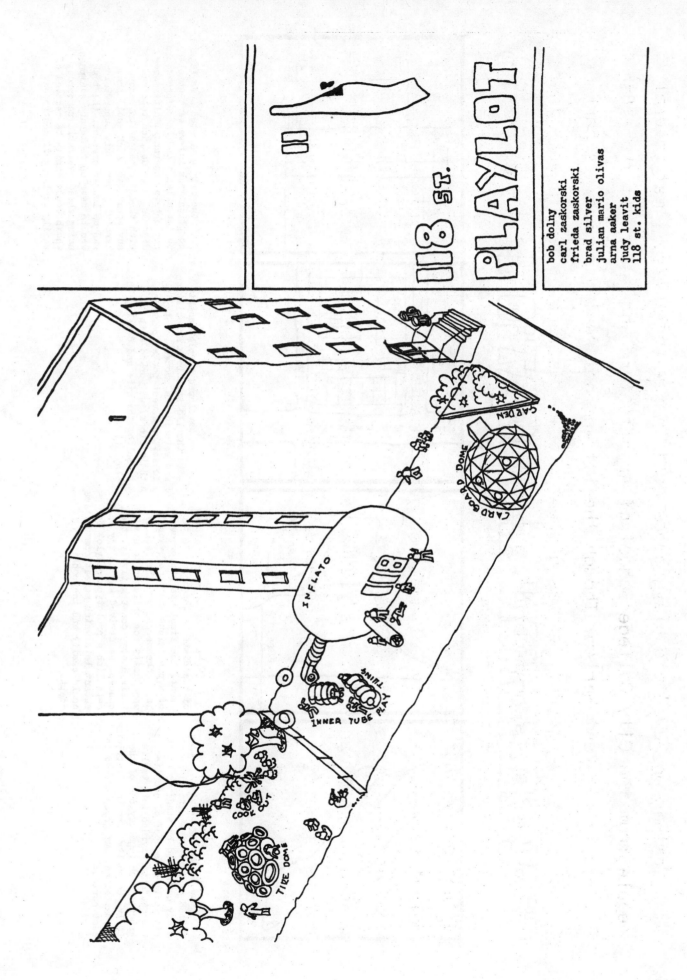

118 ST.
PLAYLOT

bob dolny
carl zaskorski
frieda zaskorski
brad silver
julian mario olivas
arna aaker
judy leavit
118 st. kids

SITE SELECTION AND LOCATION

PLATE 2

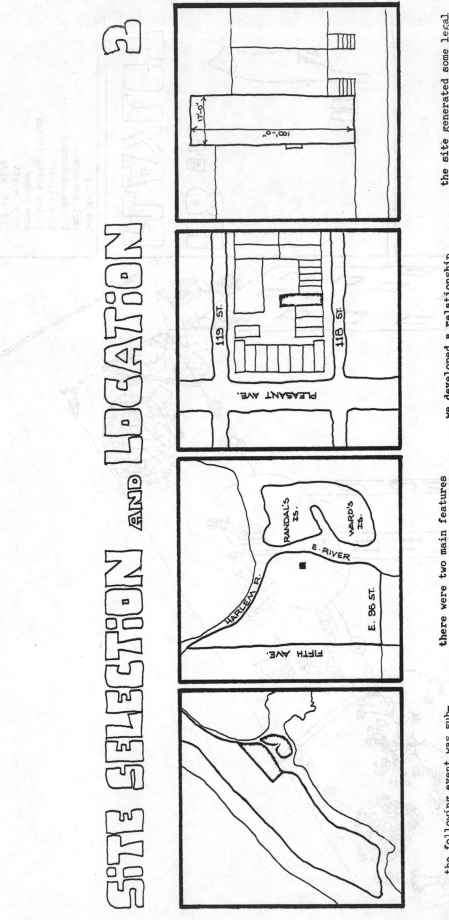

the following event was submitted as part of a site planning study conducted by students at the city college school of architecture the students divided into twelve groups, each to study one of the twelve community planning districts in manhattan. our group worked in east harlem.

there were two main features of the district which led to the following event. the first was the presence of a prodigious amount of vacant lots. the second was the lack of oppotunity for children to use their energy constructively. the concept we derived was to try to establish a prototype playlot for vacant lots which street communities could easily and inexpensively adapt.

we developed a relationship with the 118 st. block association who were in the process of trying to set up a vest-pocket park on their block. we worked with them to select the site and develop the playlot.

the site generated some legal complications and we were unable to get a lease and therefore could not obtain insurance. after some discussion we decided to squat with the requirement to remove any apparatus which would prove harmful after adult supervision was no longer present. the task was to develop temporary equipment using cheap available resources whcih could easily be removed or easily replaced if destroyed.

SITE PREPARATION

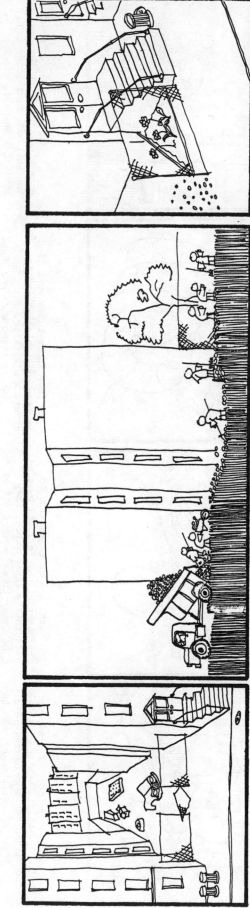

the site was typical of most vacant sites in east harlem. it was full of debris left from the demolishing of the building which once existed there. the lot served as a garbage disposal system for those apartments whose windows were lucky enough to face the site. it was also a favorite among dogs.

the group then organized work days when members of the block, predominately children would volunteer for certain tasks in site preparation. aside from cleanup routines, we conducted a search of neighbors to determine what resources we ha available. the washburn wire co. operated a factory on the block and we recieved $100.00 from the union for the purchase of gravel to cover

unfortunately the gravel arrived when no supervisors were present so the ten cubic yards of gravel were dumped on the sidewalk. so with one wheelbarrow two racks, three shovels and 100 community man hours we distributed the gravel over the lot. the gravel covered approximately 75% of the lot and we were able to construct one small hill. the

rear 25 feet was dirt and soil to allow for planting and play.

4

RESOURCE : INNER TUBES

we somehow got our hands on ten new york city bus inner tubes which measured three feet in dia. when inflated. we thought that bus or auto inner tubes would be available and a good playlot resource.

carl led an expedition to the gas station, followed by nine kids toting inner tubes. they (the inner tubes) were a bit of a problem in the street because of broken glass they couldn't be roled.

four inner tubes were tied together with clothesline to create a plaything. two or three kids could get inside and roll down the slope in the lot.

things got a little rough. some kids insited on jumping on top while it was rolling and would get squashed underneath. no one was hurt seriosly but we learned that activities involvin motion requires more space than was available at 118st.

RESOURCE: CARDBOARD 5

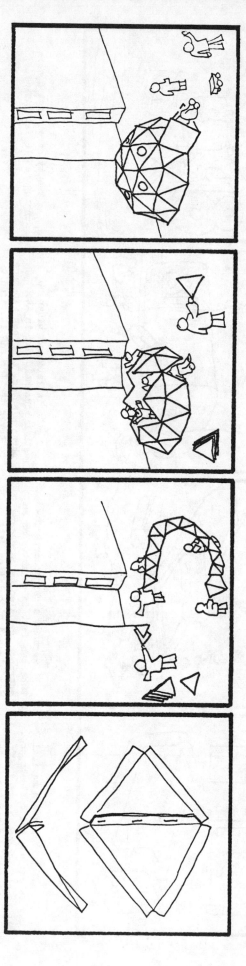

we got about four dollars
worth of 4'x8' single ply
corrugated cardboard sheets.
we cut forty triangles for a
prefabricated cardboard dome.

the dome was built by the
kids. the flaps of each panel
were stapled together. the panels
were coded and with a little
help the kids had their dome.

the dome was a temporary
structure whcih didn't stand up
as well as the others but it
provided the kids with a problem
that they worked out pretty much
for themselves.

when fully erected it was
mobbed by all the kids but later
in the day you could find one or
two kids quietly observing the
outside activity. it was the
only real private space in the
playlot.

RESOURCE : POLYETHELYNE

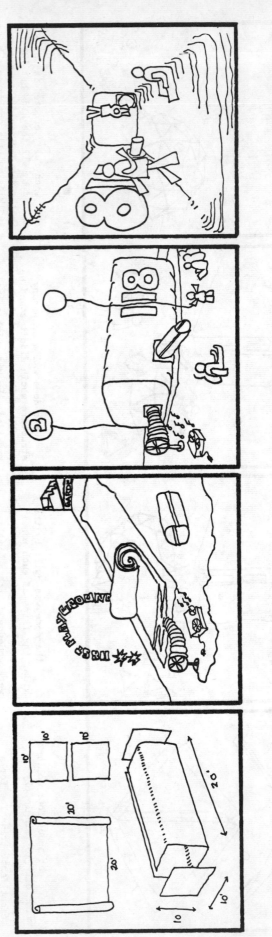

inflatables are a magical way to enclose and define space. it is also cheap. we used .006 mil polyethelyne plastic worth about seven dollars.

the patterns were cut and the seams were made with an iron. the inflatable took about six man hours to prefabricate.

we used a cardboaer sono-tube two feet in diameter as an entrance and also as an escape for air and circulation. the inflato was clear plastic with decals cut out of black plastic and heat sealed on with an iron.

the inflato was blown up with a household fan in about three minutes. a screen was made to cover the fan and electronic music was piped in through the tube which the fan used.

twenty screaming; dancing; singing people fit inside.

186

old auto tires are a great playlot resource. they give and bounce when used in astructure. they are easily available and best of all they are free. we used fifty at the playlot.

we built a tire dome as one of the remaining playthings on the lot. the dome is actually a cone shaped grid of tires supported by loose tires stuffed inside.

we used bolts and washers for connectors. holes were easily drilled in the tires for the bolts and also for drainage.

an easily made tire dome is a good thing for a playlot. kids can't get hurt. the dome can withstand outdoor conditions extremely well.

what can happen to a tire? if it gets stolen you just get more.

Double Duty for parking Lots

After Warnaco Corporation of Bridgeport, Ct., converted one of their surplus parking lots into a regulation-sized basketball court for neighborhood youngsters, it hired Meadowlark Lemon of the Harlem Globetrotters to conduct a basketball clinic. There are plans to flood the court in the winter to provide a hockey rink. With some planning, working lots can be put to the same use in the evenings and on weekends.

Minutes after the last car leaves a company parking lot for the day or weekend, "instant playgrounds" can be erected. Sockets for basketball pipe stands can be preset in the blacktop. The low concrete car bumpers can be raised and redesigned to form benches and activity dividers as well as serve their workaday function of separating cars. Plastic wading pools can be set up in minutes. Mobile play equipment can be wheeled into place and anchored in seconds. Just about the only manufactured items I endorse in this book is the mobile stuff which is too difficult to be built by amateurs, yet serves a real purpose in areas that need playgrounds immediately. Blocked off streets and unused parking lots can best be served by this sort of equipment.

The inner city company, perhaps, can hire a man from the neighborhood to help operate the temporary or part-time playground. The pushcart man with his hot dogs and sauerkraut would be very welcome in the lot. Movies could be projected on a white-painted wall during the hot summer nights. A stage wheeled into the parking lot could accommodate a dance or a rock band as well as a street theater group.

There may be definite economic advantages to a company which allows its parking lot to be used in this way. For companies generally exempt from their taxable properties that which is devoted to community use. If you're interested in the after-hours use of a parking lot, talk to the lot's owners about this tax saving!

Rokugo Tire Park

& the Playgrounds of Ota-ku

A plan for the Traffic Park in Ota-ku.

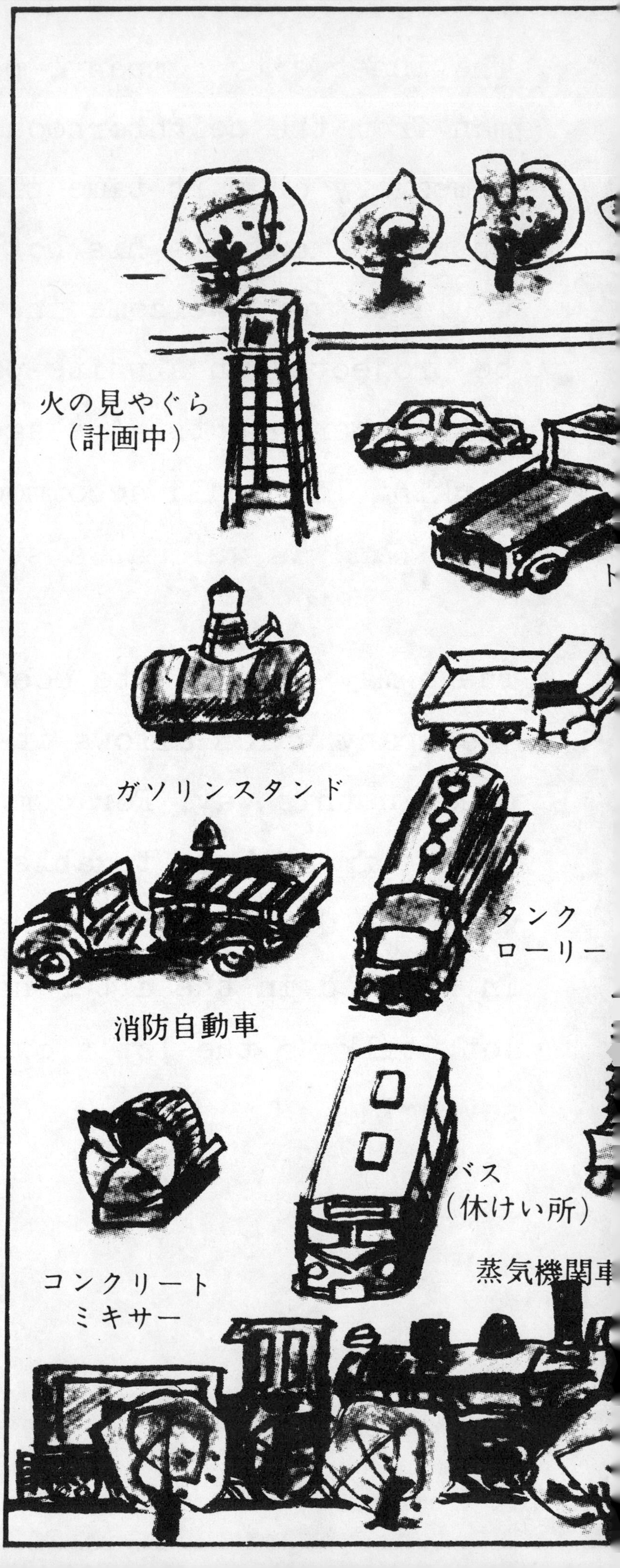

火の見やぐら
（計画中）

ガソリンスタンド

消防自動車

タンク
ローリー

コンクリート
ミキサー

バス
（休けい所）

蒸気機関車

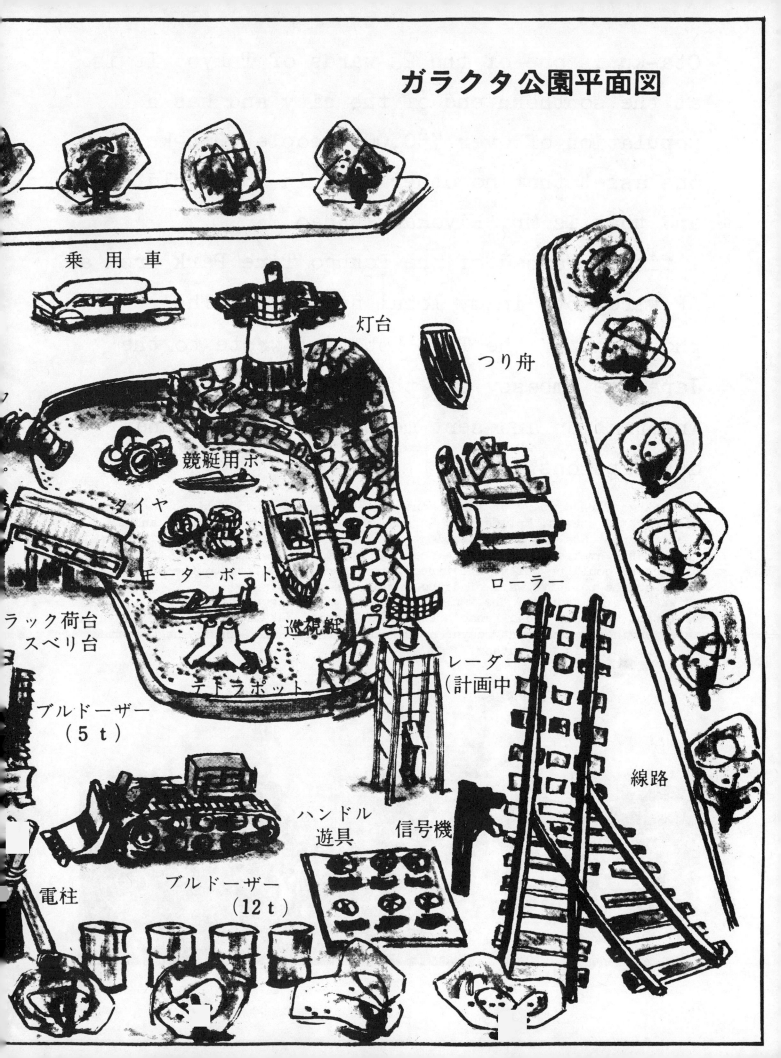

ガラクタ公園平面図

Ota-ku is one of the 23 wards of Tokyo. It is at the southern end of the city and has a population of over 750,000 people. Ota-ku has one asset that no other city in the world has and that is Mr. Kiyokazu Nanao.

I first learned of the Rokugo Tire Park from an AP wirephoto in my local newspaper. The photo was of the Tire Robot. I wrote to the Japanese Embassy and they quickly gathered information and sent me photos, plans, and descriptions.

The Rokugo Tire Company of Tokyo contributed more than 3,500 tires to the Tire Park of Ota-ku. Mr. Chotaro Suyama, a vice-president of Rokugo and a councilman of Ota-ku, was instrumental in making the tires and technical skills (plus cash) available to the engineering department of the ward so that the playground could be built. The tires were a great liability to the company, which sought positive ways of disposing of its wastes.

Shown above in front of the world's greatest tire dragon is Nanao's assistant Mr. Sado Yoda, Nanao's secretary Michiko Nakatogawa, and then chief engineer, now deputy mayor of Ota-ku, Mr. Kiyokaza Nanao. The person with the beard is the author.

I soon packed up and took the Brazil Maru
for the three-week trip from San Francisco to
Yokahama, where I was to meet Mr. Nanao.
At the time, Mr. Nanao was chief engineer of
Ota-ku - all the wards in Tokyo have their
own budgets, police, schools, street and
other departments. Now Mr. Nanao is deputy
mayor of the ward, but still keeps his hand
in playground development.

The plans for the famous Dragon of Rokugo Tire Park show it to be more than a
do-it-yourself item. But a city could build such a creature out of tires.
Who knows, maybe a big tire company might help out.

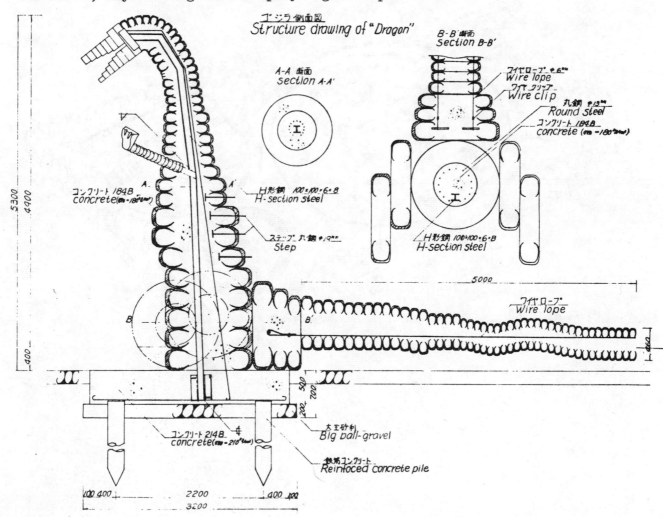

A ward councilman and vice president of the Rokugo Tire Company, Chotoro Suyama, had donated the tires and some funds to help construct the Tire Park.
While the huge slide, the dragon, and the robot are complicated and obviously costly, they are warm and beautiful works of practical play art. The more than 3,000 loose tires are continuously used in hundreds of ways.

A drawing of the Rokugo Tire Park.

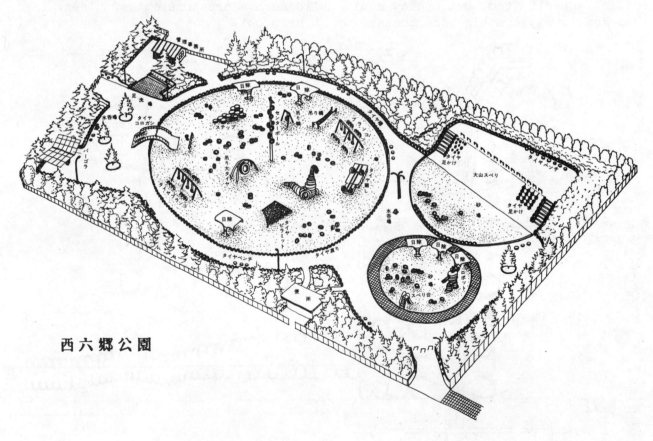

西六郷公園

Other industries helped develop the Traffic
Park and the Maritime Park and other playgrounds
throughout the ward. Ota-ku provides a perfect
example of industry cooperating with a large
city recreation department to build playgrounds
which children come to and use.

In no other playgrounds in the world have I seen
such well-integrated play. Old and young, boy
and girl - all play together in harmony.

A pile of tires can be a house, a climber, or anything you want. Not visible
in this photo are the metal culvert pipes inside the tires to keep them in
place.

There is a staff at each playground and cleaning, picking up, and maintenance is constant. Since no trash has a chance to accumulate, the children never develop the attitude expressed by "What's one more tin can - there are already a hundred strewn around."

A young fireman in a small playground in Ota-ku.

Mr. Nanao and I still write and exchange ideas. If ever you visit the Far East, stop in at the Ota-ku playgrounds made from used materials. Mr. Nanao will be glad to show you around.

Boats, piers, giant concrete jacks used for beach erosion protection, a lighthouse, and lots of loose tires on six inches of sand provide an appropriate maritime playground in Ota-ku.
What industry is your town or state famous for? What are your industries' by-products? How can you get their surpluses? Whay not go into partnership with your industrial neighbors? You can help yourself and them at the same time.

Once, the city planner Ralph Seligman asked
me to go up to Hoboken to give the town fathers
some ideas on a large playground building
contract. I suggested involving the three main
industries of Hoboken. The shippers, truckers,
and railroaders all could have provided the
materials for different playgrounds, using a
railroad theme in one, shipping in the second,
and trucking in the third. The people

Mr. Kiyokaza Nanao, deputy mayor of Ota-ku and designer of the Ota-ku
playgrounds, is seen in suit and glasses beside the huge tire swing filled
with children.

of Hoboken - the most densely populated
square mile in America - didn't want to
match federal funding for recreation, so the
whole thing fell through. And the railroad
cars, cabooses, and ties, still stand idle.
There are lifeboats, bollards and bitts (the
posts on piers and ships between which the
mooring lines are run), cargo nets, reels,
anchors, etc., all over the place. There is
every sort of truck you can imagine; there
are tires, pallets, platforms - hundreds of
items - just polluting Hoboken.

The only other oil tank truck I ever saw in a playground was in Philadelphia;
this one is in Ota-ku.

Corporate Involvement

What do you do with one of the largest springs ever manufactured when it has a minor flaw and won't pass inspection? Alco Spring Company donated one of theirs to the Jones Memorial Community Center in Chicago Heights, Il.

In much of this book I excoriate the
"establishment" - cities, politicians,
corporations - for their shortsighted views.
That the views of the powers that be need
<u>not</u> be shortsighted is amply illustrated by the
preceding description of Rokugo Tire Park.
The parks of Ota-ku are perhaps an epitome of
enlightened civic and corporate "response-
ability." Yet Ota-ku is by no means the only
example. Most of the heavy playground equipment
shown in this book could not in fact have been
installed without the use of the augers, drills,
saws, materials, etc., provided by various
utilities and commercial outfits; nor would
those tools be of much use without the men to
use them, who the companies sent out to help.
Yet there are pitfalls. As with other aspects
of playground-building, planning and ongoing
community involvement are essential. In a
previous chapter, I told of Warnaco's
conversion of a surplus parking lot into a
basketball court. But Warnaco also recognized
that playgrounds and basketball courts need

A very fancy but economical sand box was built in the old part of Amsterdam (near Nieumarkt) from "restrollen." The poles are actually the center cores from a plywood plant. After the cores become too small for the mill, they are used in many different ways for constructing playgrounds. The Amsterdam Public Works Department treates the poles before using them. What ever happens to the plywood cores in this country?

maintenance if they are to survive. They have
kept the court in first-class working order
for several years now and accept the long-term
commitment to the neighborhood. Their basketball
court was not just a one-shot publicity stunt.

Less than a mile away from the Warnaco court, at Hull House Community Center, Southern New England Bell Telephone committed itself for one day by building a very nice playground made from new and used utility poles. The company came in with its unique tools and connection devices. At work were mechnical cherry pickers, super augers and highly skilled crews; a lot of good will was generated that day. The only problem was that there was no plan to operate the playground on the second day. Community spirit was low, and no assurance of support was forthcoming from either public or private sources. Thus, the day after Ma Bell moved out, apathy, disunity, and general disaster began to move in. It wasn't too long before the lot looked worse than before the one-day spectacular. Few things are quite as dispiriting as a broken-down, neglected playground.

A very elaborate use of restrollen is seen at this playground near a Dutch
housing complex.

If you can make industry see the value of
participating in your playground plan, you
have a good head start. But even before you
approach industry for help, you should have some
plan for operation, staffing, and maintenance.

A good example of corporate involvement, in Harrisburg, Pa. A city-owned vacant lot off Norwood Street was converted to a playground by means of a combination of the resources of the neighbors, Bell Telephone of Pennsylvania, DCA, and the author.
Shown reviewing the plans are Jere Engle, City Recreation Planner for Harrisburg, the author, Josine Osborne, State Park and Recreational Advisor, and John Menapace, Manager of the Harrisburg Community Relations Service Team for Bell Telephone.
The site is ideal. It is less than an acre in area and is completely surrounded by homes; there is no auto traffic, and considerable neighborhood participation. What is more, the City of Harrisburg has agreed to participate by providing a play leader and doing periodic clean up and maintenance.
Bell of Pennsylvania gave a lot of the equipment and lent the use of their hole augers and cranes to set the heavy poles.

Industry can help in hundreds of different and valuable ways. It can also help itself at the same time. It can donate the surplus materials it produces and can't sell. It can donate the use of surplus land it's not using. It can lend the services of skilled technicians that the community could not otherwise obtain. It can lend facilities and equipment; and give all sorts of materials which can't be used by industry but have a very positive value to the community.

Pacific Gas & Electric Company provided all the labor, materials, and tools to install the poles, cargo net, and cableway for the Milpitas adventure playground built by the Milpitas School-Recreation Department in California.

When the parents wanted to add equipment to the Florence Street playground in Sharon, Pa., the Dusquense Power and Light Co. lent their heavy equipment to set out a pole horse. Four young jockeys help guide the horse into place.

Aside from the altruistic value of such corporate involvement, the hard-cash value of such participation in the affairs of the community is something that businessmen will want to consider. Remember those tax write-offs!

The story of the lot next to Hull House Community Center in Bridgeport, Ct.
This is an example of good corporate intentions gone awry. Ken Tarlow of Hull
House designed the facility and the Southern New England Telephone Co.
volunteered the equipment, men, and materials. The playground was built in just
one day, but because there was little community support and no plans or budget
for maintenance or follow-through, the play site began to fall apart on the
second day.
Unless you have a strong community organization or a realistic budget from
public or private sources, you should forget about a community playground.
The only thing worse than no playground is a playground that has fallen apart
from neglect or apathy. Plan ahead!

One major city in Texas has developed an exciting plan to maximize the use of corporate land. The city's assessors worked out a five-year tax relief program for companies that develop playgrounds on their corporate property. Thus, when a company has tentative plans for expansion, it can buy adjacent property. Not having the sales or cash potential to expand immediately, it can construct a minimum-cost playground and lease it to the city for one dollar a year for five years. The city then operates the playground. If, at the end of the five-year period, the company does not build on the property, the playground is turned over to the city, lock, stock and seesaw. If the company does build, it has the advantage of not paying taxes in an era of expanding land values. The city has benefited either way. If the land is built on, the city has had a free playground for five years. If the company doesn't build, the people get a playground free for keeps.

Sample Letter of Solicitation

The Locust St. Players
1437 Locust Street
Main City, Anystate

Anystate Electric Corp.
Main City, Anystate

Gentlemen:

The Locust Street Players is a group of concerned neighbors who are working to improve the several vacant lots in the 1400 block of Locust Street. We need help.

We are not looking for money although we wouldn't turn that down. What we really are looking for is materials. We have a design for a merry-go-round and an elevated tree house for the site. These things are designed to be made from large surplus cable reels. We understand that you might have some available which don't have to be sent back to the factory for deposit refund.

We are enclosing a copy of our plans and would appreciate your help and advice. We have a pickup truck available and could come at your convenience to receive the reels. You'll make a lot of children happy, and since we are a nonprofit organization, you can deduct
you can tax-deduct the gift of materials to our group.

Sincerely,

Mary Jo Lewis, Chairperson, Playground Committee.

212

Sample Press Release

This Saturday, Neighbors, Incorporated, begins construction on
the empty lot at 5th and Market streets in town. After long
negotiations with the City Redevelopment Authority, the local
improvement group obtained rights to clean up the debris-littered
lot and construct a playground.

John Murry and Lisa Rosenquist have been the main driving force
behind the idea of utilizing the local eyesore for the common
good. Main Town Electric has promised to donate a dozen poles
and the use of their auger truck to sink the poles for a tree
house. National Tires Service is bringing over a dozen large
"off-the-road" tires for the site. The city recreation department is lending their dump truck and bulldozer to help clean
up the trash which has accumulated for more than ten years.

Besides the residents living in the immediate area, the Boy
Scouts and Girl Scouts will spend their time helping out and
also gain their ecology and civic service merit badges. The
playground will be constructed entirely out of used and surplus
materials. The art students of Local U. have drawn up some plans
which Neighbors, Inc. are using. Come on out on Saturday and
don't forget to bring your shovel.

Here are some of the things that can often be obtained for free and used in playgrounds -

From utility companies:

telephone poles   freight cars
cable reels   pulleys
anchor bolts   turnbuckles
railroad ties   pipes
old phone booths   cabooses
loan of heavy equipment   etc

From local, state, and federal governments:

old lifeboats   ropes
cargo nets   wheels
granite paving blocks   gears
fire engines   wheelbarrows
old trucks   small tools
benches   marble steps
trees   paving slates
shrubbery   paving brick
carts   etc
loan of equipment

From private companies:

concrete   huge packing crates
plastic hose and materials   pumps
shovels   tanks
chutes   drums
slides   barrels
lumber and nails   etc

214

Concrete

Turtle Play grounds

Here is a photo of a childless playground built by a large city's recreation department. The rocket ship cost $1,896, the submarine $878, the arch $644, and the Muscleman climber $956. Another $1100 can be figured for installation, which brings the cost to a little over $5,000.

Is a playground evaluated on how low the maintenance cost is per year or on how many children use it x number of hours a day?

Think what could be done if the $5,000 went to a concerned and talented human being who could build with the children!

Like the ostrich, the turtle is an animal that hides its head at trouble. I wonder if it is this characteristic that endears the concrete turtle to so many of those people who are in the position of equipping our playgrounds.

© the New Yorker

This photo was taken at 11 a.m. at 22nd and Lehigh Avenue in Philadelphia on Washington's Birthday. It was sunny and pleasant and a school holiday.

The apologists of concrete turtle playgrounds
think it's really great that recreation
officials in their towns manage to expend
thousands - sometimes hundreds of thousands -
of dollars annually on the newest equipment
concocted by the manufacturers.

Three minutes later and one block away, I took this photo of Top Cat's
playground. By the time this book appears, the City will have destroyed Top
Cat's playground. Will the kids vandalize the other site to even the score?

They wax enthusiastic about outsized abstract
bees to climb on or crawl through.

They ramble on about simulated rocket ships,
the various flying flapdoodles, and all the mass
produced items that fill dozens of catalogs.

These same apologists wonder, that, in Philadelphia, for example, playground vandalism takes a $100,000 chunk out of the annual recreation budget. I wonder that it's not more! With one side of our mouths we preach "good old American rugged individualism," bootstrapping and "do it yourself if you want it done." Yet we really make a mockery of these phrases when our recreation boards sit in executive session at night and pore over the catalogs and choose what they think the children will like.

While the basic idea of surplus land utilization for playgrounds, either permanent or temporary, is a sound one, it is essential that city governments or neighborhood groups spend a few dollars for a part-time neighborhood staffperson to clean up the place every once in a while and work and play with the children. Half an hour a day would be enough to keep this Chicago playlot in shape.

A photo of the "creative" playground at the Osaka World's Fair. Fifteen
minutes after the lovely bridge was opened up for children to scramble over,
it had to be closed, due to numerous injuries. I tried to climb it myself and
almost broke my neck. Most of the other stuff in the nightmare playground
was soon broken or closed down. The rest of the Fair was great - the
children's part, terrible.

The solution to vandalism is almost too
simple. You just give people a part of the
action. You help them build for themselves.
We forget this simple truth, "that which we
create, we protect."

The fence around this Philadelphia miniplayground presents an interesting obstacle to the vandals who hold up the stage every day. Since there's no people to stick up and no gold, the kids just throw rocks.

A senior citizens' park in West Philadelphia.

I spoke one night at a PTA and when I got on to my least favorite subject, the concrete turtle, the audience laughed. I asked the group why the laughter. One person got up and told me they had bought a 400-pound turtle a few months before. It was, after ten minutes, ignored completely by the children. Then one night, the turtle took a walk and was never seen again!

I'd guess that playground equipment has an annual sales close to a billion dollars. This doesn't include essential items, such as basketball setups, bats and balls, etc. I do feel that 90 percent of the industry could close down tomorrow. If those left without jobs went into playground leader's jobs, the whole country would be better off. Whole new schools to train such leaders could develop and in a few years the tide of vandalism could change to a tide of participation.

This well-built city playground in Baltimore uses a lot of dead trees and used materials. It's just across the street from an elementary school. The street is closed to traffic most of the day, so the whole area is a great big playground.

Nursery Playgrounds

Many books have been written about nursery
schools but very little has been written about
the nursery-school playground. I know, from
working at the Charlestown Playhouse in
Phoenixville, Pa., for one day a week for ten
years, how important the playground is.

These two young race drivers are off to a flying start in a Maine nursery school.

It's a fun place, but a learning place as well.
So many, many schools and nurseries lack such
simple items as blocks of wood, hammers, and
nails. The Charlestown Playhouse has work
benches, paints, all sorts of tools, trikes,
wagons, and blocks.

This plane at the Charlestown Playhouse, Phoenixville, Pa., is made from an old crate and some 2 x 12 planks. The water faucet is a unique radiator mount.

Meanwhile, on the other side of the world, an Aeroflot jet, made of old wooden planks, clears for takeoff from the nursery school in Akademgorodok, Western Siberia.

As a memorial to Oskar Stonorov, a major landscaping job is now (1974) underway at the Playhouse. We plan to install three water faucets so each age group can play in mud and water. There is already a fire pit and once a week the children cook hot dogs and learn to respect and use fire in a proper and safe way.

The secret for a good nursery school playground
is just about the same as for any other sort
of playground. Just keep your eyes open.
Always drive with an empty trunk so you
can fill it up with the goodies you pass by
every day.

The packing-crate house at the Charlestown Playhouse. The fathers painted the
realistic books and furnishings and even installed a nonworking sink.

Almost anything can be used. Foam packaging
boxes are great. Old wool, spools, cardboard
boxes and tubes, plastic milk cartons, old
photographs - if you can't find a use for
them, the children will!

This natural sculpture made from a tree root is the focal point of the Little
Red Brick Schoolhouse nursery school in Litchfield, Ct.

This log summer toboggan is at the Kinderspielplatz in Vienna.

When asked to help with the playground at the Serendipity Center, the first thing the Playground Clearing House workers did was cut a lot of holes in the high fence so the children could look out at the beautiful creek flowing by.

This photo taken in a nursery school playground in New Zealand shows a practical use of an old dead tree.

A track made of 2 x 12 planks with a 2 x 4 center guide makes a nice roller coaster for Timmy Horn at the Charlestown Playhouse. Old casters are used for wheels, which are mounted on the end of a box.

By building their own seesaw out of a sawhorse and a plank, the children of the Charlestown Playhouse learn some of the principles of balance, as well as of cooperation, while having a good time. Bob Ciaco and Jason Rose are shown finding their own particular balance point.

Two views of the SUECEC playground designed and built by Walter Tryon's students. (See Page 234 for a description of the SUECEC project.)

Children of the Charlestown Playhouse assemble a peg and hole construction assembly invented by the author. The idea is good, even though the toy manufacturers didn't think so. If anyone wants to use this construction toy for free - be my guest.

I built this slide for the Phoenixville, Pa., Day Care Center several years ago. The slide is 18-gauge stainless steel, and was assembled as described on page 46. The cable reel acts as both stand and guard rail.

I also built this sun and rain shelter at the Phoenixville Center. Make sure you use bolts rather than nails. With children climbing all over, there must be strong, yet flexible, connections. Nails become loose in a few weeks and the whole thing will fall apart.

Thinking About Playspaces

The following is from a letter sent to me by Walter M. Tryon, Instructor in Landscape Architecture at the State University of New York (SUNY), Syracuse.

In May of 1973, a playground was designed and constructed for the children of the Syracuse University Early Childhood Education Center, SUECEC, by the Students and Faculty of the Third Year Design Class at the School of Landscape Architecture, College of Environmental Science and Forestry, SUNY, Syracuse. SUECEC was established with the intention to provide a place of research and observation for the university staff and students. Children from the ages of three to six attend this Center throughout the school year. SUECEC philosophy recognizes the innate ability of the child to teach himself or herself through experience. No one method of instruction is employed; rather, teachers are encouraged to experiment and adopt teaching methods suitable for the individual child.

The Center's physical space is designed to meet this philosophy. Instead of organizing activities for specific times during the day, space has been allocated according to general behavior:

1. The Expressive Area provides for the child's creative potential with paints, cardboard, sand, water, etc.

2. The Active Area has no restrictions on noise level and allows for un-restricted large muscle play.

3. A child in the Task Area can use the small didactic toys, listen to a story, or pursue any other quiet activity.

In the spring of 1973, SUECEC investigated the possibilities of extending the child's learning experience in addition to offering the opportunity for outdoor play. The School of Landscape Architecture was contacted and the design and construction of a learning play environment was initiated as the semester project for the Third Year Design Class. The project was organized into three phases:

1. Data Collection
   a. Site Characteristics
   b. Child Behavior
   c. Available Free and/or Inexpensive Materials
   d. Design Criteria
   e. Program Development
2. Design and Jury Selection
   a. Individual student's design solution submitted.
   b. Six of the 75 submittals chosen by the class.
   c. Jury of SUECEC Staff and Landscape Architecture faculty selected
      the solution that best reflected the SUECEC philosophy and design
      criteria.
3. Construction
   a. Development of detail, design, and construction drawings.
   b. Confirmation of donations and purchase of materials.
   c. Student participation in site construction.

The completed playground has a central focus created by a circular multilevel
sand structure (see photos). This form is reinforced on the ground plane by a
hard surface that allows for free movement of tricycles and carts. Adjacent
low platforms set in a gravel base provide an area for sitting, quiet play,
group reading, etc. Five trees are placed strategically around the area, and
are considered part of the play environment. Another large sand area is
bordered by timber rounds set vertically at different heights. In an effort to
visually and physically integrate the playground, a climbing structure
consisting of swings, ladders, and decks connect the lower area of the site
to the natural hillside.

A graphic mural designed in large geometric forms and bright primary colors is
painted on the wall of the building.

The value of the playground extends primarily to the children of SUECEC; yet
to those who participated in its design and construction, the playground also
represents an educational experience and a rewarding expression of commitment.

Michael Ryder sits in peaceful repose inside a huge tire sunk into the ground at the Me Re Center, Gresham, Or. There is a beautiful hollow echo when you sing in these rubber caves. Notice the wood chip floor.

Special Education

Bill Mack, Yale art student and straw boss of his school's project at the New Haven Regional Center for the Mentally Retarded, is shown on the entrance tower making final adjustments to the play machine. The assembly was designed both as a recreational device and a training machine to help children of the center develop their mental and motor skills.

The play machine was built by first-year architecture students, and many New Haven companies and craftsmen donated materials and time to the project. What is your local college planning for its projects? There is often a vast fund of muscle and knowledge just a phone call away.

Every child has the right to an education, no matter how limited the child's ability to learn. Responding to this right is said to put a heavy demand on the taxpayer; and school districts in the past tended to ignore or even hide the retarded or physically handicapped children.

I've built perhaps a half-dozen playgrounds
for physically and/or mentally retarded
children. In most cases, I followed the
same procedure in planning, design, and
construction as I do for regular playgrounds.
I prepare a slide demonstration for the children,
the parents, and the teachers. The adults would
try to elicit a response from the children
wherever possible. Where the children are unable
to verbalize, we try other ways of gauging
their reaction to the various slides we show.
Clapping or ohs and ahs or even excessive
disturbance in the audience would indicate
the preference of one play item over another.

Joyce Ridge, Director of the Arizona Preschool for Retarded Children, watches
children play on a cement sculpture built by the fathers of the students. The
skeleton was of 1/2-inch reinforcing rods; metal lath wired onto the rods hold
the mortar. The mix should have two parts sand with one part cement and one
part lime so that it will stick to the mesh until it sets.
By letting the children participate in the construction, you let them develop
needed motor skills and have fun at the same time.

Naturally, I'd consult closely with the parents, teachers, and administrators about the particular needs and abilities of the children and be guided accordingly.

At the Western Montgomery Special Education School in Spring City, Pa., I had a most rewarding time. As in most special schools, the children and parents come from every background and from a wide range of financial and educational attainment.

At Spring City, on the work day, bankers dug ditches with truck drivers. Stockbrokers and unemployed laborers worked side by side installing heavy concrete pipes. The mothers dug and pushed as well; and mixed up in the whole chaotic day were the children, who tried to help to the limit of their ability. We could have worked twice as fast without the care of watching the children. We couldn't lay an ax or a saw down, but had to stow them safely away so that the children wouldn't harm themselves on the dangerous (for them) tools.

While this indoor play site at the Arthur Goldberg Center was not designed specifically for mentally handicapped children, the use of cardboard carpet tubes, rope, and indoor/outdoor carpeting make for an ideally soft playground. The inner tube swings give a "floating on air" sensation.

GI's from Fort Benning volunteer their off-duty time to help at the Listening Eyes School in Columbus, Ga. Most of the children have special radio receivers and loudspeaker earphones and can't play as roughly as they would like. These tire swings look like they'd support an elephant. (See page 27 for another photo taken at this school.)

The tree house at the Me Re Center is super safe and easy to get to. Heavy railings protect the children who still get a thrill out of being up in the air.

I built a more elaborate tree house sliding board for the Western Montgomery Special Education School in Spring City, Pa. At first, the rail went completely around the porch. I thought it would provide a good hand grip for the children, to swing under. But the children were so intent on going down the slide that they often hit their heads on the rail. So I cut it out and installed heavy corner braces. Now the children slide down and no head hitting has occurred.

Twelve feet of donated culvert help develop the crawling skills of Douglass Fullerton. The pipe is padded with indoor/outdoor carpeting.

Doris Norton, teacher at the Me Re Center, helps Matt Thompson on one of three sets of balance beams of varying width, which are used to develop coordination skills.

But it was worth the delay and extra effort.
The children had a sense that people and adults
loved them and were working with them. The
parents, who all had that most basic of common
denominators - a handicapped child - planned
and worked together, and a very special
playground was erected.

Most of the play items shown in this book
can be adapted to the needs and abilities of
handicapped children. A letter by Joyce Ridge
of the Arizona Preschool for Retarded Children
excerpted in this chapter attests to this fact.
Nor should we be over-fearful that handicapped
children will be harmed by exciting play. On
a recent trip to London, I visited Lady Allen
of Hurtwood. The world's leader in the adventure
playground movement couldn't wait to show me her
latest creation - an adventure playground for
retarded children.

When we drove up to the school where the
playground was located, I noticed that it
was set back several hundred feet from the
road. Before I had a chance to comment on this
inconvenience, a car pulled up, a teacher
took a child and put her in a sort of breeches
buoy. The child was propelled with a mighty
push and with a happy scream went flying down
the monorail to the landing platform inside
the school. The "landing officer" shot back the
breeches buoy for the next child. What a
wonderful way to go to school! The whole
system was just a series of connected
garage door rollers. The rail was covered,
so there was no problem with rust or dirt.

We must multiply the examples shown in this
chapter a thousandfold, and find ways to
allow handicapped children to participate
in building and experiencing their own
environment to the limit of their capabilities.

The railroad tie steps to this wide slide are covered with indoor/outdoor carpeting to protect the children who fall while climbing.

A long shot of the tire refuge. The outside can be to climb on; the inside is just to be in.

This merry-go-round at the Developmental Center for Autistic Children developed from the bolts available. I had four bolts 38" long, so I put two reels together to make up 37". As it turned out, the pipes on top make very good hand grabs.
The basic plans for this merry-go-round are shown on page 10. When the thing starts to squeak, it needs a little oil.

This tree house basement, two feet deep in foam rubber, is in the world's first adventure playground for retarded children, located in London. It was designed by Lady Allen of Hurtwood, the leading authority and advocate of adventure playgrounds. The children climb a ladder to the tree house and then drop through a trap door onto the foam below.

This cable reel seesaw was built by a father of one of the children attending the Western Montgomery Special Education School in Spring City, Pa.

Thinking About Playspaces for Retarded Children

The following is from a letter by Joyce Ridge of the Arizona Preschool for Retarded Children.

...At the Arizona Preschool we are hoping to build a fort of our sandbox from utility poles - making it a kind of peanut shape - with the height going from short to tall. There will be steps to enter by. We hope this more enclosed area will greatly increase sandbox play.

We have also cut shapes - squares, circles, and rectangles - from old plywood, painted them with bright colors (paint donated), and hung them on the fence. We will do shape, chalk, and paint boards also to hang.

An old ladder painted has provided great help for children with poor coordination. They love to walk through it - at first they need some help.

Tires were set in concrete, with iron rods to hold them. Several sizes were made so those who had problems could use the smallest first. Size and number concepts were also helped by this. And, of course, we also hung tires and some were stacked in piles.

Other very much enjoyed additions have been old telephone wire spools - these were sanded and painted. They are in constant motion and have helped greatly in hand-foot coordination as they are rolled. They have also served to strengthen muscles on many of the children as they roll the heavy ones around. They are also great for balance as the children climb on them.

Now for our play sculpture: the children have enjoyed it so much more with the bright colors on it. One of the greatest gains has been the increase of group play - it provides an area where several can play, whether it be together or side by side. It has also provided good opportunities for mastering the skill of walking up steps, ramps, crawling, and imaginative play with the use of the holes. It cost us nothing to build as we got the materials donated, and the actual building was done by one of our dads and a group of college students.

First, you need a load of waste sand from a contractor. This is then molded into the shape of the general design; after you work with the sand and have a pretty good idea of what design you desire, you cover it with chicken wire. Cement is then poured over the top, covering the chicken wire and sand. The holes are made by placement of tin cans. The whole structure must be allowed to dry for about one week before you dig out the sand - by far the hardest job! We've since used the sand for other work projects...

We have also had some bean bag throws made by a 5th grade class at a local school. A basketball shoot made by some YMCA boys will also be a new addition. It will be made so that we can alter the height and also I used a bright waste paper basket instead of a net - to make it easier for the children to see and aim at.

WMSEC PLAYGROUND

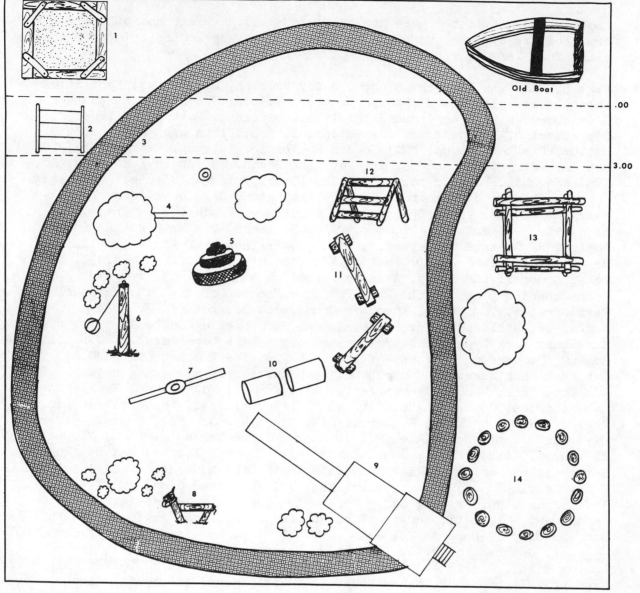

Old Boat

.00

3.00

Brick Wall

1	Sand Box	8	Horse
2	Steps	9	Tree House
3	Brick Walk	10	Concrete Pipe
4	Swing	11	R R Tie
5	Tire Tree	12	Log Ladder
6	Tether Ball	13	Log Fort
7	Seesaw	14	Reading Circle

Designer - Paul Hogan   Artist - E. Bloomquist

Picture Credits

Photographs not listed here are by Paul Hogan. Drawings not otherwise credited are by Carol McChonochie. Unless otherwise noted, pictures are cited from left to right.

Page 5, Oil City Derrick. 6, top, Nancy Rudolph, Educational Facilities Laboratories. Bottom, Michael O'Donnell. 7, top, Sue Levy; Arizona Republic; Greensboro, N.C., Parks and Recreation Department. Bottom, Philadelphia Department of Licences and Inspection. 8, top, Pittsburgh Post-Gazette. Bottom, Charles Baccus, DCA; Gordon MacKenzie. 10, top, George Pohl. 10, bottom, 12, bottom, and 13, top, Jo Anne Hogan. 15, Arvid Bengtsson. 18, Appleton, Wi., Post-Crescent; William Loewe, Chicago Tribune. 19, Luanda, Angola, Chamber of Commerce. 20-21, Wilmington, De., News-Journal. 22, Nancy Koran. 23, Peter Spooner. 25, Salisbury, Rhodesia, Department of Amenities. 26, unknown. 27, top, Palle Hestbech, Danish Foreign Ministry. Bottom, Al Alexander, Columbus, Ga., Ledger-Inquirer. 28, top, William Meyer, Milwaukee Journal. Bottom, Vic Condiotty, Seattle Times. 31, bottom, Peter Spooner; Sue Levey, Arizona Republic. 33, top left, redrawn from Canadian plans in the Park Practice Program of the U.S. National Park Service. Top right, Theodore Osmundson. 35, bottom, Jo Anne Hogan. 36, William Owens, Philadelphia, Pa., Evening Bulletin. 37, top, Nuremberg Park Department. Bottom, Honolulu Park Department. 38, top, Jo Anne Hogan. 39, drawing courtesy of the Park Practice Program of the U.S. National Park Service. Contributed by Canada; from a drawing by W. L. Breti. 40, top, Brian Woods. Center left, David Kuroda, Educational Facilities Laboratories. Center right, City of Philadelphia. 41, top, Matt Herron. 42, 43, M. Dudley. 44, Hoyt E. Carrier II, Grand Rapids, Mi., Press. 49, top, Owen Cartwright, Nashville, Tn., Banner. 61, center and bottom, Michael Parkhurst, Ithaca, N.Y., Journal. 62, and 63, top, Educational Development Services. 63, bottom, SWEAT Associates. 65, Robert Grant, Grand Junction, Co., Daily Sentinel. 66, left, Louisville, Ky., Courier-Journal and Times. 67, left, John High, Jr. 68, Nancy Koran. 70, Salisbury, Rhodesia, Amenities Department. 71, left, Austria Foreign Office. 72, top, Arvid Bengtsson. Bottom, City of Durban. 74, Jean Lacy. 75, top, Luanda Chamber of Commerce. 76, top, Greensboro, N.C., Recreation Department. Bottom, left, Art Fabian; bottom right, Cincinnati Enquirer. 77, top, Diane Stowell. Bottom, Alton, Il., Evening Telegraph. 82, Nancy Koran. 84, Bill Keane, the Family Circus. 85, left, Owen Cartwright, Nashville, Tn., Banner. Center, Atrican Primary Science Program. Right, Karl Jaros. 87, Pacific Gas & Electric. 88, left, Duane Bradley, Minneapolis Tribune. Right, George R. Smith, Plainfield, N.J., Courier News. 90, unknown. 91, top, James Joyner. Bottom, Kankakee, Il., Daily Journal. 92, bottom, Betsy Bloomquist. 94, top left, African Primary Science Program. Right, Jo Anne Hogan. Bottom, Hoyt E. Carrier II, Grand Rapids, Mi., Press. 95, Helma Cornejo, Blue Island Il., Sun-Standard. 96, Bob Ponce, Santa Barbara, Ca., News Press. 97, Jo Anne Hogan. 98, 99, R. Miller. 101, Matt Herron. 104, Quinn, Phoenixville, Pa., Daily Republican. 105, top, Bernard Langlais. Bottom, Jean Lacy. 106, bottom right, Bob Ponce, Santa-Barbara, Ca., News-Press. 110, left, Arvid Bengtsson. Right, Minneapolis Parks and Recreation Board. 111, left, Arvid Bengtsson. Right, James Joyner. 112, John McCormick. 113, top left, Barbara O'Mahoney. Top right, Arvid Bengtsson. Bottom, Ace Hoffman. 114, Mark Perlstein, Wisconsin State Journal. 115, top, Bob Ponce, Santa Barbara, Ca., News-Press. Bottom, John McCormick. 118, Nancy Koran. 121, U.S. National Park Service. 123, San Francisco Chronicle. 126, bottom, San Francisco Chronicle. 129, Randy Trabold, North Adams, Ma., Transcript. 130, bottom, Jean Lacey. 132, right, Charles

Steinbrunner, Dayton, Oh., Daily News. 133, top, Jean Lacey. Bottom, Mark
E. Lawrence, Forester. 134, bottom left, Elenor Lacey, Pueblo, Co., Star-
Journal & Chieftain. Bottom right, G. C. Dwyer. 138-139, 140, George Pohl.
141, left, George Pohl. Right, Matt Herron. 142, George Pohl. 144, 145,
Christopher Speeth. 146, George Pohl. 152, 155, John Hyk, Jr. 156, top left,
Charles Baccus, Pennsylvania DCA. Bottom, Clair Law, Clearfield, Pa.,
Progress. 158, 161, Mark Valan. 162, Mike Viola, Philadelphia Inquirer. 169,
Royal Danish Ministry for Foreign Affairs. 170, Arvid Bengtsson. 171, Robert
McGuire. 172, Marcia Witlin. 173, Royal Dutch Touring Club. 174, Marcia Witlin.
175, left, Austrian Foreign Office. Right, Arvid Bengtsson. 176, top left,
and right, Marcia Witlin. Bottom left, Nancy Rudolph. 177, top, Marcia
Witlin. Bottom, Robin Moore. 178, top, Robin Moore. Bottom, Dennis Galloway.
179, top left, and bottom, Robin Moore. Top right, Arvid Bengtsson. 189,
190, Warnaco Corp. 192, 193, Tokyo, Ota-ku Ward Office. 194, Tokyo, Asahi
Shinbum. 195, 196, Tokyo, Ota-ku Ward Office. 203, Chicago Heights Star.
205, 207, Amsterdam Public Works Department. 208, Bell Telephone. 209,
left, Robert McGuire. 210, Bridgeport, Ct., Sunday Post. 216-217, Philadelphia,
Pa., Department of Recreation and Conservation. 218, top, B. Tobey, the New
Yorker. 220, Chicago Department of Urban Renewal. 223, Baltimore Department
of Recreation. 224, unknown. 226, Portland, Me., Gazette. 228, bottom, Nancy
Rnadolph. 229, top, Austrian Foreign Office. Bottom, unknown. 230, top, New
Zealand, Christchurch Star. Bottom, unknown. 233, John Hyk, Jr. 236, Art
Fabian. 238, unknown. 239, Phoenix, Az., Gazette. 241, top, George S.
Zimbel, Educational Facilities Laboratories. Bottom, Al Alexander, Columbus,
Ga., Ledger-Enquirer. 242 and 245, top; Art Fabian. 245, bottom, and 246,
Gail Kennedy. 247, E. Bloomquist.

Acknowledgments

I must first acknowledge the great debt I have to my wife, Jo Anne, and to
my children, Paula Hogan Whiteway, Lisa Sanders, Tieg Hogan, Evan Sanders,
Orin Hogan, and Michael, Philip, Erica, and Christopher Sanders. They have
been and are the real incentive to my building playgrounds.

Next, I must pay tribute to my own parents who gave me rare gifts - the
freedom to play as I wanted and the guidance to build properly.

Watching and working at Betty Stonorov's nursery school, The Charlestown
Playhouse, had a great influence on me. From the time my first child went
there, I was fortunate enough to participate in all the activities of the
school. It is a cooperative school; and I spent a great deal of time building
with the children as part of my work obligation. Elsewhere in this book I
talk about work done amongst and with these children.

If Betty was my inspiration, Oskar Stonorov was my mentor. I respected
Oskar and was challenged by him hundreds of times. I count and cherish the
few times I bested him; I cherish as well the times I did not, and they
were legion. I was in Moscow when I heard that he went down in flames with
his friend Walter Reuther. I miss the intellectual combat with Oskar that
helped drive me on. We were friends.

Karl Linn and Milton Shapp have influenced and helped me. Karl, with his knowledge and extraordinary ability to inspire, organized my random thoughts on what playgrounds should be. Milton has backed me privately and publicly for more than a dozen years. He has endorsed my ideas to city councils and state legislatures when many scoffed at the idea of children building their own playgrounds.

Lady Allen of Hurtwood, the world's leading figure in the adventure playground movement, has been an inspiration to me. On my visits to London, she has always taken time to show me her latest work. The last time I saw her she took me to the first adventure playground for handicapped children.

Scores of other people around the world have knowingly and unknowingly contributed to this book. The head of the Chamber of Commerce in Luanda, Angola; the Director of the Amenities Department in Salisbury, Rhodesia; my Intourist guide in Khabarovsk, Siberia; Robin Moore of the Berkeley School of Environmental Design; Morris Dudley, the Director of Parks and Recreation in Corpus Christi, Texas; and hundreds of others I either met or corresponded with have aided me.

I must give special thanks to William Wilcox, Secretary of the Pennsylvania Department of Community Affairs, who has enthusiastically backed my Playgrounds for Free program throughout the state.

I've devoted an entire chapter to the work of Kiyokazu Nanao, the Deputy Mayor of Ota-ku, Tokyo. While chief engineer of this ward of 750,000 people, he conceived and constructed a half-dozen unique playgrounds, among them the Traffic Park and the Rokugo Tire Park. He was a warm and generous host, as was the vice president of the Rokugo Tire Company, Mr. Chotoro Suyama.

I must praise VISTA and its dozens of volunteers who helped me build so many playgrounds in the regions of Pennsylvania devastated by Hurricane Agnes.

Volunteers Granger Brown, Judy Shatzoff, Andy Pellettieri, Fern Apfel, Dave Loechel, Carol Patch, and many others gave their time and love to help children and communities rebuild their lives. Without their help, little could have been done for the thousands of children who lost their homes and were moved to impersonal trailer parks.

The Pennsylvania Bureau of Recreation and Conservation, as a whole, was supportive of my ideas. In particular, I thank Bill Gohdes, who manned the Erie District. Bill always looked forward to leaving his desk and digging ditches with the children of his region; he is now working with me full-time.